HIGH ARCTIC

BY GEORGE MIKSCH SUTTON

High Arctic. New York, 1971.
Oklahoma Birds. Norman, 1967.
Iceland Summer: Adventures of a Bird Painter. Norman, 1961.
Mexican Birds: First Impressions. Norman, 1951.
Birds in the Wilderness. New York, 1936.
Eskimo Year. New York, 1934.
The Exploration of Southampton Island, Hudson Bay. Pittsburgh, 1932.
An Introduction to the Birds of Pennsylvania. Harrisburg, 1928.

ILLUSTRATED BY GEORGE MIKSCH SUTTON

A Guide to the Birds of South America (in part). By R. Meyer de Schauensee. Wynnewood, 1970.
Reptiles of Oklahoma (in part). By R. G. Webb. Norman, 1970.
The Birds of Arizona. By Allan Phillips, Joe Marshall, and Gale Monson. Tucson, 1964.
The Birds of Colombia (in part). By R. Meyer de Schauensee. Narberth, 1964.
Fundamentals of Ornithology. By Josselyn Van Tyne and Andrew J. Berger. New York, 1959.
Georgia Birds. Norman, 1958.
A Guide to Bird Finding, West. By Olin Sewall Pettingill, Jr. New York, 1953.
A Guide to Bird Finding, East. By Olin Sewall Pettingill, Jr. New York, 1951.
World Book Encyclopedia (section on birds). Chicago, 1941.
Birds of Western Pennsylvania. By W. E. C. Todd. Pittsburgh, 1940.
The Golden Plover and Other Birds. By A. A. Allen. Ithaca, 1939.
American Bird Biographies. By A. A. Allen. Ithaca, 1934.
The Birds of Minnesota (in part). By T. S. Roberts. Minneapolis, 1932.
The Burgess Seashore Book (in part). By Thornton Burgess. Boston, 1929.
The Birds of Florida. By H. H. Bailey. Baltimore, 1925.

HIGH ARCTIC

AN EXPEDITION TO THE UNSPOILED NORTH
by GEORGE MIKSCH SUTTON

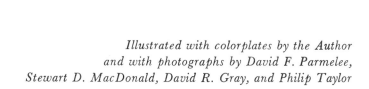

Illustrated with colorplates by the Author
and with photographs by David F. Parmelee,
Stewart D. MacDonald, David R. Gray, and Philip Taylor

PAUL S. ERIKSSON, INC.
Publisher
New York, N.Y.

Endorsed by the Laboratory of Ornithology, Cornell University.

DEDICATION

Grand men named Fridtjof Nansen, Vilhjalmur Stefansson, Louis Bement, Clarence Wyckoff, Donald B. MacMillan, Frederick A. Cook, and George Hubert Wilkins, all of them important in the annals of arctic exploration, were friends of mine. Some of them I came to know well. Half a century ago I gave Nansen and his lovely daughter a guided tour of the Carnegie Museum in Pittsburgh—all because the museum's director knew that I loved the Far North. Cook, a controversial figure if there ever was one, came to visit his friends, Clarence Wyckoff and Louis Bement (each of whom has a far northern cape named for him), while I was on the faculty at Cornell. What a night we had—hour after hour of reminiscing until full daylight! MacMillan, grateful for my interest in a school he had established on the Labrador, named some islands after me. They are not important islands, but I know they are beautiful. For Stefansson, a rugged creature we all called "Stef," I wrote a voluminous piece about arctic birds—an opus that should never be published for it is full of errors and hopelessly out of date. Hubert Wilkins, an ornithologist at heart, I knew during World War II. He as a civilian, I as an officer in the Air Corps, were sent to the Aleutians to test survival equipment. Adrift in a life raft, we timed the dives of oldsquaw ducks in Casco Cove off Attu. We had little else to do, actually, our chief aim being to survive.

May this book, unimportant though it be in "the annals," honor the memory of these men.

FOREWORD

When I was fourteen or fifteen years old I got stuck for a wretched hour or so while crawling through a hollow log in Texas after a turkey vulture's nest. The log lay in a north-south direction. Held fast near the south end, I realized that I could not back out. The only way to go was forward, i.e., northward. Finally, after a long stretch of pushing, pulling, and loss of buttons, I got out. Friends like to say that my love for the far north must have stemmed from that boyhood experience. The north end of that log did seem, I must admit, a part of the world most decidedly worth reaching.

I have gone northward—"down north" as the Labrador livyers say—several times. In 1920, as a member of the four-man crew of the Grenfell Mission's 45-foot motor yawl, *Northern Messenger,* I went down the Labrador from Battle Harbor to Cape Chidley, very close to the northeasternmost tip of the North American continent. Three years later, with a Carnegie Museum party travelling in freight canoes, I descended the great Abitibi River to Hudson Bay. In 1926, again with a Carnegie Museum party, I went down the Missinaibi, across James Bay, down the east coast of Hudson Bay as far as Richmond Gulf, and then, in a Revillon Frères schooner, the *Albert Revillon,* through Hudson Strait and "up" the Labrador coast to Rimouski, Quebec. In 1928, an expedition to the North Shore of the Gulf of St. Lawrence, I met Sam Ford, a Chief Trader of the Hudson's Bay Company. This man knew a lot about blue geese. He had talked with Eskimos who had actually seen the nests of blue geese at a place called Cape Kendall. He promised to help me reach the nesting ground if I'd come to his post on Southampton Island for a year. So to Southampton I went in the late summer of 1929, there to learn first hand what Hudson Bay, the "world's icebox," could be like in winter.

My love for the North Country did anything but die as a result of that wonderful experience. In the spring of 1931 I went to the mouth of the Churchill River, along the west coast of Hudson Bay, to help find the nest of the Harris's sparrow, a bird I had seen much of on its wintering ground in Texas. In 1932 I went to Saskatchewan, in 1934 to British Columbia. As an Air Force officer in World War II I was sent to Alaska and the Aleutians. Satin-white Attu, at the western end of the great Aleutian chain, was among the most beautiful places I had ever seen.

In 1953, eager to push farther north and to show a promising graduate student what the North Country was like, I went to Baffin Island, taking David Freeland Parmelee with me. What a summer we had—cold, gray, wet, at times discouraging, but all very exciting!

In 1956 I returned to Hudson Bay, this time to paint pictures for W. E. Clyde Todd's forthcoming *Birds of the Labrador Peninsula,* an opus to which Mr. Todd had devoted a lifetime. My headquarters were at the Hudson's Bay Company post, and there I stayed most of the time; but a hard-bitten pilot named Rusty Blakey flew me across James Bay to Rupert House. Not far from the Ontario-Quebec border we looked down on a moose family—a great bull, with immense antlers, a cow, and a little calf, whose meal was not to be interrupted by any bird, be it ever so large or noisy, that might circle over. At Rupert House I talked with Mrs. Mavor, about whom I had heard (through Mr. Todd) for years. "Indeed I remember Mr. Todd," said Mrs. Mavor. "Who ever in this world could forget *that* man!"

In 1958 I wanted to go to Siberia, but correspondence led nowhere, so I decided to go to Iceland instead. The birds of Iceland interested me greatly, but I came

vii

away feeling that it was the country and its people rather than the birds that I would remember.

In 1962, some important tables turned. This time it was Dave Parmelee who did the inviting. With him I went to Victoria Island, where for the first time in my life I saw yellow-billed loons in full breeding plumage. I even drew day-old yellow-billed loon chicks direct from living models. In 1966, again at Dave's invitation, I went to Jenny Lind Island, where I painted all summer long—save for one quick trip to the Ross's goose breeding ground south of Queen Maud Gulf. I painted lesser snow geese, jaegers of all three species, light-bellied brant, king eiders, golden and black-bellied plovers, a stilt sandpiper, glaucous and Thayer's and Sabine's gulls, a pair of rock ptarmigan, a snowy owl's nest, and a family of Lapland longspurs. Jenny Lind was not very far north of the Arctic Circle.

Men who have lived along the shores of the North Polar Mediterranean refer to all southern islands of the Canadian Arctic Archipelago and to all northern parts of continental North America as "the banana belt." They use this phrase scornfully.

Year after year I had realized that for all of my talk about the "far north" and its wonders, I'd never even looked down on the High Arctic. I had been a miserable visitor to the miserable "banana belt." So when Dave Parmelee and "Stu" MacDonald asked me to go with them to Cornwallis, Bathurst, Ellesmere, and other really far northern islands, what could I do but go? I'd have been faithless, even—in a way—dishonest, if I hadn't.

George Miksch Sutton

Norman, Oklahoma
June, 1971

*Long-tailed
Jaeger,
Bathurst Island*

*Long-tailed
Jaeger,
Bathurst Island*

Colorplates

Photographs

*Note: A direct-from-life *drawing* of a Collared Lemming in *winter* pelage will be found on page 55.

HIGH ARCTIC

In the early spring of 1969 my friend Stewart D. MacDonald, Curator of Vertebrate Ethology at the National Museum of Natural Sciences in Ottawa, invited me to go with him to Bathurst—a big island northwest of the north end of Baffin Island about half way between the Arctic Circle and the northernmost lands known to man. Officially, as part of the museum's expedition, I would be affiliated with the Polar Continental Shelf Project, sponsored by the Canadian Department of Energy, Mines, and Resources. My special province would be the behavior, life history, and distribution of arctic shorebirds—an avian group in which I had long been interested; but I would be expected to do some painting, too.

I had heard much about Bathurst Island from David Parmelee, who had been there with MacDonald the preceding summer. The island had muskoxen, Peary's caribou, and wolves; I'd never forget what I'd heard about those wolves. The arguments "Stu" MacDonald used were persuasive: we'd be there for only a month or so; camp was already established and in operation; there'd be no guns, ammunition, or food to order; all I'd have to do was gather up my painting outfit and come.

For a time I demurred, since I had promised to help with proofreading an important book on the birds of Guatemala. But when word reached me that galleys could not possibly be coming my way for weeks, I decided to go to Bathurst. I flew from Oklahoma City to Ottawa on June 2; by jet from Montreal

*"The faculty took a kindly interest in the
undergraduates. There were no student uprisings."*

*Faculty and student body at "Bathurst Academy" on 21 June 1969—
the day after Parmelee's birthday. Left to right: Danks, Byers, Taylor, Sutton, Parmelee,
Gray, MacDonald, Lamothe. Each man was on the faculty and
each—in a "high arctic" sense of the words—was an eager undergraduate.
Note the horned Snowy Owl in Parmelee's hands.
Photograph by Stewart D. MacDonald, whose face, alas, is masked by shadow.*

The Bathurst camp on 11 June 1968. The Parcoll hut to the left is referred to as the "old Parcoll" in this book. The "new Parcoll" is slightly upslope to the right. Photograph by David F. Parmelee.

to Resolute, Cornwallis Island, on June 5; and by Otter from Resolute to Bathurst on June 7.

The Otter was badly crowded. Aside from Stu, Dave, and me there were two entomologists, Hugh Danks and Robert Byers; luggage for the five of us; supplies for camp; and a big husky named Tuka, who won me over completely (and slobbered over me almost as completely) by quieting down when I put my arm around her neck in the noisy plane. Finding camp was a problem, for our pilot had misplaced his map. Stu recognized certain topographical features and when a man in camp let fly a great piece of orange-colored cloth, down we came, graceful as a gull. The ease with which we alighted astounded me. There was no violent jarring or jolting. The ski equipment worked perfectly.

Camp was along the eastern side of the island at the end of a smooth, snow-covered ridge ten miles inland from the head of Goodsir Inlet. The three men there—David Gray, who was making an intensive study of muskoxen; his assistant, a French Canadian named Pierre Lamothe; and Philip Taylor, a senior at the University of Alberta in Edmonton—were living in a red "Parcoll" hut. About fifty yards south of the Parcoll was the white canvas cook-tent. Slightly upslope west of the Parcoll and cook-tent were "the makings" of a second Parcoll. By the time our gear had been placed inside the "old" Parcoll there was no room for anything else. The other hut was sorely needed.

For me the coming into being of that second Parcoll was little short of miraculous. The floor and metal framework were already in place, so an important part of the work was done. The north wind was relentless; but the sun had long since climbed above such mundane problems as those concerned with rising and setting,

5

so there was plenty of light and to spare. Everyone fell-to wholeheartedly—uncrating, unrolling, stretching, and fastening in place the tough, two-layered rectangles of weatherproof fabric. The gradual nascence was, in its own technological way, as romantic as that of my first Aivilik Eskimo snowhouse back in the fall of 1929: the hum of coordination and camaraderie; the puffing and wheezing and blowing on fingers; the tightening of cords and clicking of metal snaps; eventually the adding of a storm-porch at the front and a sweeping of snow from the floor.

I must be honest about my part in all this. What I did was tinker—pull a little here, push a little there, tie knots, and grunt. The grunting was not done for effect. I really felt like grunting!

I tried to help with the moving. Carrying my long fibre suitcase, which caught the wind badly, I got about half way between the "old" Parcoll and the new when I found myself badly short of breath, stumbled in the snow, lost balance, and fell. Embarrassed, a little frightened, and oddly thankful that no one had seen me, I got up and started on; but a strong hand took the suitcase as Stu MacDonald said: "That's for me, Doc. Let the young folks do the work. Remember those fingers of yours. They must be kept in shape for painting." Breathing heavily inside the new tent, I was frank in admitting that I was badly out of shape and in expressing wonder as to why I should be feeling giddy. Not a syllable from anyone hinted of disappointment, disillusionment, or annoyance. Even as I tried to figure out what I *could* do to help, I sensed a feeling of concern, of respect, of comradeship—a feeling that was to continue week after week at that friendly spot.

6

A partly built Parcoll hut. Photographed at the Bathurst camp by David F. Parmelee in the early summer of 1968.

MacDonald, Parmelee, Taylor and I set up housekeeping. Our Parcoll was, like the "old" one, sixteen feet square and about eight feet high. It faced north. The north and south walls were vertical, the other two strongly curving. An oil-burning stove was at the south end. There were four windows, two at the north end, two at the south, each double—two panes separated by an insulative layer of air. I chose the northeast window and corner, for here the light promised to be good for drawing. Stu made a table for me by nailing a square of plywood to a box. Each of us had a cot. Between my sleeping bag and the springs were *two* foam-rubber mattresses. For this embarrassment of riches I did my best to be doubly grateful.

It was after all that construction work was done, in the middle of the night, that I had my first look at free-ranging wild muskoxen. Through a telescope standing in the snow at the northwest corner of the "old" Parcoll, I watched them. David Gray was with me. What I saw appeared at first to be two boulders, a large one and a small, black against the snow. The cold wind gnawed at my face. I could not keep my eyes free of tears for more than a second or two at a stretch, but presently I perceived that the larger boulder had become two, and that all three boulders were changing shape slowly. I was spellbound. What I was seeing was so genuine, so unembellished, so reduced to absolute verities!

The muskoxen were about two miles away, foraging for willows and saxifrage under the snow. They kept their heads down, so there was no telling which end was which, and occasionally they lined up in such a way as to appear to be only one. "There are four," said David Gray. "They're moving toward us. That's why you can't tell much about their shape. I've been watching them for several

"Those remarkable animals . . . Why did I feel so deeply about them?"

Two adult bull Muskoxen on a favorite feeding ground in low country between Signal Hill and Triangle Point northwest of the Bathurst camp. Photographed on 22 June 1969 by David F. Parmelee.

days—three bulls and a cow. They spend most of their time in that part of the valley and on the slope just west of Eeyore Hill."

David was a graduate student at the University of Alberta. He had been at camp since late April, giving all of his time to studying muskoxen. He had been on Bathurst during the summer of 1968, too. He planned to overwinter, if possible, and to base a doctoral dissertation on his findings.

Seeing those muskoxen, fully realizing that the blunt, shaggy creatures were actually they rather than a nicely composed photograph, and that I was actually I, gave me a feeling of completeness, of fulfillment, that I have rarely felt. Since the fall of 1920, when I had begun to consider myself an authority on things northern—for about fifty years in fact—I had been thinking and reading about muskoxen, mentioning them in lectures, showing pictures of them to classes, discussing them as if all that I said were based on personal experience. I had never told an out-and-out lie about them. I had never said in so many words that I had hunted them or watched them form a circle with heads out, horns ready for action. But my voice had had the ring of an eye-witness's, and I had made no effort to modulate that ring. What I was seeing now, in that lovely white valley, was far more than four muskoxen. I was seeing part of myself, too—an ambitious, self-centered, sometimes ruthless part that had failed to make clear that it had never seen a wild muskox anywhere. A justifiable accident that might happen to anyone? A pardonable desire to be considered authoritative? No, neither justifiable nor pardonable. How could anything short of complete honesty and complete humility be acceptable in the presence of creatures and habitat as noble as these?

As I looked through the telescope, my eye eagerly sought for certain detail. How much of the horns was actually visible? Was that hump on the back flesh and bone, or was it mostly hair? My eye worked hard, for it had much to see. My mind worked too, for curiosity was reaching far, far beyond such trivial matters as shape and color. How had the species muskox managed to survive? This wind; this glare of whiteness that forced me to wear dark glasses; this snow that covered food; the fierce cold; the wolves; the nine months of winter, year after year, decade after decade! Why had not the inexorable process of natural selection eliminated muskoxen long ago? How could they be co-existent with me, inhabitants of my world? They were so obviously part of a by-gone age—the smoldering embers of a fire that had refused to go out. I was genuinely puzzled and deeply moved by the simple fact of their being where they were at the moment, of their living presence near me.

As David Gray told me more of what he had observed, I realized how little, how very little indeed, I had known about muskoxen. Having read that the animals ate grass, I had come to believe that no grassless part of the arctic could support them. "They eat lots of willow," explained David, handing me a willow tree possibly a century old that had stood three or four inches high and fanned out over a square foot or two of ground before he had pulled it up with its roots. "They chew their cud, too. Even when they're quite a long way off, you can hear their stomachs rumbling."

This unexpected statement led Stu MacDonald to tell us of an incident on another of the big arctic islands: "We were in country that had lots of musk-oxen. One evening while my companion and I were pitching camp near a narrow

Four
Muskoxen
travelling
toward their
feeding ground
below
Signal Hill,
Bathurst Island

*Four
Muskoxen
travelling
toward their
feeding ground
below
Signal Hill,
Bathurst Island*

stream, we observed that two muskoxen a hundred yards or so beyond the stream showed no alarm. We considered moving, for we didn't want the animals to mistake our tent for a rock and begin rubbing themselves on it. When, after supper, we saw that the muskoxen were still there, our misgivings continued; but we'd had a long hike and were pretty tired, so we turned in. I went to sleep promptly, but was wakened by stomach rumbling so loud that I was sure the muskoxen had arrived. Half asleep, I got up, realized we didn't have a proper paddle, club, or stick to our name, and perceived that all the rumbling was right there in the tent—in the other sleeping bag."

At our first full meal together in the cook-tent, everyone agreed that the season was exceptionally late. Snow was everywhere. The river had shown no sign of cutting loose. Hillside trickles had little more than started. Sanderlings had not yet arrived. No one had seen a saxifrage blossom or a bumblebee. A wolf had passed through our camp recently—almost certainly "Old Bloodface," the very animal that had killed a full-grown muskox single-handed—a killing witnessed through a telescope from start to finish on May 28, 1968, by Dave Gray. No, there had been very few hares and caribou near camp, but there had been plenty of lemming sign, and Phil Taylor had found nine snowy owl nests. In 1968 there had been very few owls and virtually no lemmings. Could facts of this sort be related? MacDonald and Parmelee agreed that camp had fairly hummed with the cries of courting ptarmigan, sanderlings, and knots in the spring of 1968. Where were all these birds now? Could lateness of season be solely responsible for

"Could all the gray young ones have been captured by predators?"

Young Arctic Hare in the gray pelage worn by this species during its first summer. Fully adult Arctic Hares of Bathurst, Ellesmere, and other high arctic islands remain mostly white the year round. Photographed by David F. Parmelee not far from the Bathurst camp on 12 August 1968.

their absence? Thinking back over my own experience on the coasts of Hudson Bay, on the Labrador, and on Southampton, Baffin, Victoria, and Jenny Lind islands, I realized that I had never been in a far northern camp that had been as silent as this during the second week of June.

I begged my companions to set me straight about certain place-names they continued to use. Across the broad valley north of us was the low dome they called Eeyore Hill. There, a year ago, Stu, Dave Parmelee, Phil Taylor, and a man named Cy Hampson had watched a bull muskox die, apparently of old age. The bull had wandered slowly to the hill, by himself. There he had stayed, day after day, always alone, becoming—in Parmelee's words—"something of a landmark, because he was always there." Stu decided to name him Eeyore, after the hapless old donkey in Milne's *Winnie the Pooh*. Approached by two-legged creatures bearing cameras, Eeyore would run a short way, about-face, rub a foreleg with his nose as warning that he was about to charge, and back up against a steep bank. One day the men at camp noticed that Eeyore was down. When, an hour or so later, they saw that he was still down, they crossed the valley to find out what was wrong. Eeyore lurched forward, but could not get up. As he lay on the ground his eyes protruded, becoming wonderfully translucent, like polished moonstones or agates. For about two hours he lay there, virtually motionless save for an occasional attempt to get up and the slow lifting and sinking that accompanied labored breathing. His human friends, saddened by his utter helplessness, stood by to the end. What was left after his last gasp they examined carefully. His teeth were worn down to the very gums.

Eeyore Hill had been important otherwise, too. An arctic hare that had had a nest very close to camp surprised everyone by leaving her brood frequently, swimming the river, and making her way across the valley to Eeyore Hill to feed. Time after time Stu and the others had watched her leaving the hill, swimming the river, and returning to her brood. They even had photographed her while her hungry foursome were having a meal of thoroughly masticated, well digested, biochemically transformed, properly emulsified saxifrage blossoms. She had continued with this daily routine until the river had become too big and rough for her to swim.

Beyond Eeyore Hill was a deep valley, almost a gorge. A mile or so farther on, and directly north of camp, was a huge black boulder that remained free of snow all winter—North Star Rock. Well to the left of this important landmark was Hare Ridge, and well to the right Skull Rise. The last of the eminences to the eastward was Signal Hill.

Between camp and all these places was the Goodsir, a sizeable river too deep for wading when full, but icebound, buried with snow, and invisible now. Running eastward across the whiteness below camp was a curving dark line of gravel on which wind never allowed snow to gather—the river's south bank. The low country east and south of camp would be marsh, dotted with hundreds of ponds, when the snow went. Off to the southwest several miles was "the big lake" for which there seemed to be no other name—now a vast expanse of weathered ice. Not far from the lake were two great rocks called the Laughing Heads. These had been named by Parmelee who had been obliged to walk many miles toward them when a motorized vehicle had suddenly bogged down in soft snow. Parmelee's thoughts had become less and less pleasant as he had trudged toward the

Purple Sandpiper

rocks. Getting the vehicle back to camp might require the help of aircraft—an expensive operation. Without the vehicle the whole camp would be crippled. All this time wasted—walking, walking, walking—while he could have been covering new country if only that blasted vehicle . . . When Parmelee had finally reached the rocks they had seemed to be laughing at him. His name for them had stuck.

On the morning of June 8 I wakened early, conscious of having slept well. Observing that my tent-mates were still asleep, I rose quietly, put on my warmest clothing, and went outside. The wind was sharp. A deep drift of snow had formed south of the tent. Tuka, who had escaped from her rope halter, ran swiftly toward me, crouched when a rod or so off, and crept forward whining, as if begging forgiveness for sins of whatever sort, whether committed or not. Remembering my own shortcomings, I rubbed the deep fur between her ears and the whining stopped.

From 7 to 9 o'clock I wrote notes. These were jumbled. Too much had been happening. I consulted my watch, wondering whether I'd slept a whole day, then decided that it must be morning since the sun was high and scintillant. When Taylor awoke, he whispered good morning and brought me his notebook. We communicated *sotto voce*. What we said must have been interesting, for the two sleeping bags at the south end of the hut joined the conversation. At about 10 o'clock we had breakfast in the cook-tent—hot porridge, rye crispies, assorted jams and jellies, and some of the best butter I ever ate.

Dishes out of the way, everyone squared off for work. David Gray bundled up, put food in a knapsack, shouldered telescope and tripod, and announced that he was heading for "the other side of the valley." This might mean, I was to learn, that he'd be gone two hours or ten. His black-eyed, black-bearded, lanky assistant, who had been following muskoxen around all night, was sound asleep. How anyone could be sure when night ended and day began was beyond me at the moment.

MacDonald and Parmelee assembled equipment, intent on finding rock ptarmigan for Stu, who was studying that species' courtship behavior, and sanderlings for Dave, who probably knew more about sanderlings than anyone else on earth; who had banded several adult and young sanderlings near camp the summer before; and who was determined to find some of his banded birds. Complete with heavy parkas, boots, dark glasses, guns, cameras, binoculars, tape recorders, and parabolic reflectors, the MacDonald-Parmelee team looked like Abercrombie and Fitch window mannequins hung with everything "outdoorsy" worth mentioning. *How do they keep track of it all?* I wondered.

Phil Taylor's interest focused on snowy owls. Informed by Parmelee and me that some of the nests he'd found would almost certainly contain nine or ten eggs eventually, and that eggs would be laid not daily but about 48 hours apart, he was somewhat non-plussed. A nest that had held four eggs on May 25 had recently been deserted; at that nest the first egg could have been laid as early as May 17. Two nests that were within a mile or so of camp held only three or four eggs each at the moment. These two nests he could visit daily, perhaps several times daily, but making the rounds of eight nests might prove to be im-

possible, especially later in the season when the river would be difficult to cross.

Hugh Danks and Bob Byers unpacked microscopes, collecting nets, phials, glass slides, and preserving fluids. Their work was to deal with the overwintering of insects and other invertebrates. Recalling how I had tried to find a hibernating bumblebee during that long winter with the Eskimos of Southampton Island, I plied these experts with questions about the instar stages of arctic butterflies and moths.

At the moment I had no freshly shot bird specimen that would serve as a model. I decided to draw from memory a fan of bare ridgetops that we had looked down on while flying to Bathurst, so I dug out my painting outfit. That first picture was a farce; but I enjoyed doing it and was glad to find that my right hand was functioning.

Of a sudden I realized that what I could see through my own window was wonderfully beautiful. I moved table, cot, and chair a bit, found the spot that afforded the best view, and got to work in earnest. The wind was bothersome. The hut rattled incessantly. Gear hung here and there shook loose and fell just as I was concentrating most fiercely. But everything held together and presently I could see Eeyore Hill and North Star Rock on the paper before me as well as through the window. In mid-afternoon I heard feet stomping and an excited voice shouting: "There go seven brant, right past Eeyore! They're the first we've seen here at camp!" I moved to Phil's window and strained my eyes. There they were, sure enough, a company of seven small, dark-colored geese, so tightly bunched that they looked like an oddly-shaped single bird, travelling swiftly westward across the wind.

As conversation concerning that most dependable of topics, tardiness of season, resumed, six sanderlings shot past the tent only a few rods from my window. Could spring be arriving at last, all at once, within a ten-minute period? "No," reported Stu, who was in the storm-porch brushing snow from his boots, "we didn't see a saxifrage blossom anywhere, not a one!"

Everybody seemed to like my drawing, especially the little black spot representing North Star Rock. I believe they'd figured that I'd miss a detail of that sort. Sharp-eyed Phil, who was comparing my picture with what he could see through the window, commented: "Maybe you could put that bull caribou in, too. He's just a bit east of what you show—sound asleep." This item I had missed. With my binoculars I made out the antlers—slender and dark against the snow, like stubby remnants of a wind-ravaged tree.

I took a walk before supper, keeping to the top of the ridge. Between the bare areas the snow was up to two feet deep and tiresome to walk through, for the crust was not firm. I found some lemming tracks, but the only birds I saw were three long-tailed jaegers that chased each other as if in play, squealing noisily.

That evening, all that night in fact, I was bothered by indigestion. The malady obliged me to hurry frequently to an uncouth structure known as "the biffy." The focal point of this architect's nightmare was an upended oil drum that was shielded from the wind by a vertical slab of plywood. Leaning against the windward side of the plywood were caribou antlers so serenely beautiful that the briefest glance at them helped. "No kidding, Doc, why don't you paint a picture of the biffy and show those antlers?" was Phil Taylor's suggestion.

The morning of June 9 was delightfully bright and calm, but toward noon the wind became its own gruff self once more, flinging the snow into long, grace-

Brant,
Bathurst Island

Brant,
Bathurst Island

ful zastrugi all over the ridge. Despite the wintriness of the scene, Pierre Lamothe reported seeing five snow buntings and a Lapland longspur in the valley north of camp.

Dave Gray gave us a blow-by-blow account of the killing of the bull muskox by "Old Bloodface"—the wolf mentioned above. The muskox was by himself when the wolf approached. At first Dave thought the wolf was merely teasing or employing "diversionary tactics," waiting for another wolf, or several wolves, to appear. But what looked like frolic and romping was anything but that: it was lethal tactics. There was no nipping at hindquarters, no attempt to hamstring. Every attack was directed at the head. The muskox swung fiercely with his horns; but the wolf—nimble, powerful, expert—danced about, waiting for an opening. Surprising his quarry with a sudden lunge, the wolf got past the horns and tore off hair and an eye. The muskox continued to toss his great head, doing his best to gore his assailant; but loss of blood and eye told on him. Finally the wolf seized the throat, and the muskox went down. The battle had lasted 53 minutes —from 8:20 to 9:13 p.m. Before leaving his kill, the wolf tore away great mouthfuls of hair, broke the ribs behind one shoulder blade, drank blood, and ate the tongue.

The graphic power of Dave's words chilled my blood. Suppose a man, alone on the tundra, is spied by a hungry wolf and taken for a muskox. Or suppose he *isn't* taken for a muskox, but the wolf comes on anyway and starts its sprightly *danse macabre*, swinging nimbly to the right, nimbly to the left, darting forward, backing up, darting in again, never pausing for more than a second or two. Suppose the man has no gun. Suppose he can't even find a rock . . .

"There he had stayed, day after day, always alone . . ."

*"Eeyore," a very old bull Muskox, a few days before his death.
Photographed by David F. Parmelee on Eeyore Hill, across the Goodsir valley
from the Bathurst camp, on 25 May 1968.*

After the wind's brief assault on the morning of June 10, the weather became remarkably pleasant. We began to feel that summer had come. I made a point of examining several saxifrage plants, confident that I would somewhere find leaves turning green or a bud opening. I looked in vain. I had to pick the dry, thickset bundles to pieces, exposing the pale, tender, hidden parts, to convince myself that they were alive. I decided to paint a whole brown plant in detail, to put down the date as evidence of spring's failure to arrive, and to add a purple sandpiper when one became available.

Why not get that sandpiper myself? The weather was fine. I would not need to walk fast, for there'd be no one to keep up with. How about those grassy spots in the low country south of camp? There *had to be* purple sandpipers somewhere on a day like this! I started off in the direction of "the big lake." I had gone about three hundred yards when I was overtaken by Dave Gray who explained, with winsome diffidence, that I was headed straight for some of his muskoxen; that he wanted to color-mark one or more of those very animals; that if I showed up suddenly I might put the whole band to flight. No one had told me that frightened muskoxen sometimes run for miles rather than forming a circle and standing their ground. I made clear that I wouldn't for the world frighten those muskoxen. I'd look for sandpipers in another direction.

At that very moment we saw the gulls—two wide-winged, soaring glaucous gulls—majestic, luminous, clear-cut against the unequivocal blue. Not a sound did they utter. Their slow circling had an almost geometric precision, as if a theorem or law were being explained by some Learned Teacher far above them. When I heard Dave's voice, when I realized that the sounds he was making were not words but something else, I could not help watching him. He was every bit as interesting as the gulls. I was moved by the way in which the brightness above him seemed to shine from his face. His eyes glowed. He looked at me as if he'd

never really seen me before; then as if requesting me to keep secret an important idea that had just been imparted to us both. I felt like saying, "Sure, David, I'll keep the secret," but of course said nothing. Is it experiences of this sort that bind a man to the far north? Are "intimations of immortality" of this sort experienced anywhere? I wonder. When Dave and I separated—he heading for his muskoxen, I turning northwestward—I was a changed, a somehow rehabilitated, person. Never again would I be quite what I had been a quarter of an hour earlier that day.

Dave's plan did not work out very well for him, though it did for me. The fifteen animals, terrified by the blast that color-marked one of them, ran swiftly northward over the ridge, their shaggy hair rippling and billowing. I'm not sure that they even saw me. When they reached valley-level they were out of sight for a while, but presently they reappeared, moving at steady speed beyond the river. Across the valley and up the slope they went toward a low saddle between Eeyore Hill and Skull Rise. On they ran, never pausing to look back, very small by this time. As they moved out of sight, miles away, they were still running.

I pulled up a saxifrage plant, walked to the tent, and got to work. My sketch was half done when Stu MacDonald came in, fresh as the wind, announcing that he'd seen *four* purple sandpipers "over toward the Laughing Heads." Sanderlings and brant one day, a longspur the next, purple sandpipers the next: spring had surely come! "I heard them twittering," Stu continued, "and one bird lifted a wing in display." MacDonald, Parmelee, and Taylor started off. No one needed to tell me where they were going. I returned to my drawing board—completely *saxifraged,* as it were.

Two hours later, while I was a quarter of a mile from camp, looking for a yellow lichen that I wanted to include in my picture, I saw three men walking toward the tent. I knew who they were. One of them was holding a small object up for me to see. I knew what *that* was, too. Parmelee did not wait for me. Despite the eight miles or so that he had just covered he walked to meet me, beaming with joy. Together we examined the specimen—a purple sandpiper that had not quite completed its molt into breeding feather. How exquisite were the ashy grays, warm browns, and purple-glossed black parts of its plumage!

My eyes were tired. I made a quick sketch that recorded the colors of the fleshy parts, put the specimen outdoors in a safe place, and went to bed.

I tackled the drawing again in the morning. The plumage patterns were intricate; but it was the saxifrage, the bits of lichen, and the thousand and one pebbles that took over. There was, indeed, too much accessory material. The picture became as much a portrait of pebbles as of sandpiper. Everyone voiced approval, saying that I had caught my subject's "protective coloration" perfectly. This was not, alas, what I had intended. There were some "good things" about what I had put down; but my next drawing would be better. I skinned the specimen, finding it to be a female—and rather fat. The ova were slightly enlarged. Bob Byers examined the stomach contents carefully, finding the remains of several caterpillars, some fly larvae, and a small ichneumon wasp. Just where had the sandpiper found all that insect food? That was the sandpiper's secret.

I insisted that I be given a "camp job," some not too onerous task that would keep me from feeling like a social parasite. Thus it came about that Pierre Lamothe and I had "KP duty" every fourth day. Now Pierre was a man of action, drive, and originality. He had memorized several recipes. What he did not remember, he improvised. Occasionally he used a cup or spoon for measuring—not because he needed to, but to show me how it was done. I admired his cavalier attitude tremendously. Being a poor cook myself, I measured meticulously; yet my biscuits tasted of soda; my muffins were rubbery; and my flapjacks were either as pale as chamois skin and sticky inside, or crisp and black. I could gather snow and put it on to melt. I was good at mixing powdered milk with water, once I had conquered the egg-beater. I learned in time to use a gadget designed not so much to open cans as to test the ingenuity of mankind. I loved to watch Pierre breaking up great handfuls of spaghetti and dropping them into scalding water. I loved to watch him flinging flour, salt, and sugar about. I mention these details for all of them were part of every fourth day. Eight men eat a surprisingly large amount of food. Preparing and eating meals put to use almost every dish and implement we possessed three times a day. Meals were great fun. The meals, not the dishwashing.

Pierre was usually nonchalant about his cooking, whether all went well or not. As a rule no one criticised what was set before him and ate regardless of inner conviction or pain. On one occasion we beheld a bewildered, a somewhat contrite Pierre; he had erred somehow in mixing the dough for "maple-syrup dumplings." The syrup had come to a boil, and the dough was there, bubbling away like one of those fearful mudpots in Iceland, but the dumplings would not integrate. They formed a thick scum and kept right on boiling—along with the syrup. We roared with laughter as Pierre spooned out what I couldn't help calling the "viscous meniscus." It is only fair to add that every bit of the stuff was eaten. It was awfully sweet and awfully good.

34

Late in the evening on June 11 four muskoxen moved slowly across the valley north of camp. I adored them. They were so wonderfully real. The sun was low, the shadows long and intensely blue. The muskoxen were on their way to a favorite feeding ground at the foot of the high country. Part of Signal Hill was in deep shadow. I could not resist the impulse to draw the scene—though up to that moment I had never dreamed of drawing one muskox, to say nothing of four. To keep the rough paper clean I made cutouts and drew with hard pencil around them. David Gray helped.

By the morning of June 12 the great thaw was on. This we knew because there was a broad dark streak running the full length of Eeyore Hill; because the ground near all three tents was wet; and because lemmings were everywhere. The pretty little rodents, forced from their burrows by water, were scurrying across the snow; sprawling like thick, tiny rugs in dry spots, enjoying the sun; or standing on their hind legs, alert for danger. Even without listening carefully, we could hear lemmings under our Parcoll. At the cook-tent two or three lemmings, all adult, came and went, one of them a battle-scarred veteran that spent much of its time near the trash can. Alarmed by an approaching hand or foot, it darted into the sanctuary between the two layers of canvas at the tent's entrance, stood up with digging claws at the ready, and made small defiant noises. A trimmer, more amiable animal allowed me to pick it up in my cupped hands while we were having breakfast. Placed on the table, it whisked about sniffing at crumbs, wiping its whiskers, and nipping fingers that came too close. Why it nipped other fingers than mine I did not understand. Probably I possess some of the ingredients that go to make up an acceptable lemming.

A Thayer's gull visited camp that day, looking for scraps, but wary. Hour after hour it stood watching the cook-tent at safe distance. I threw it one of my flapjacks, but this must have looked more like missile than morsel, for the gull lifted its head high, inspected my offering haughtily, and flew off.

On June 13 I painted a male snow bunting, using as a model a skin that Phil Taylor had prepared when the bunting vanguard had arrived in mid-May. I showed the bird singing. The rock on which it was perched Parmelee had carried in from Hare Ridge. On the rock were bright orange lichens with the charming scientific name *Caloplaca elegans*—the very epiphyte I had seen on Attu, at the western end of the Aleutian Chain. So abundant had *Caloplaca elegans* been on Attu that some of the towering cliffs there had fairly blazed when the sun struck them directly.

On June 14 I became acquainted with the motorized vehicle known as the Ski-Doo and with the toboggan that it pulled. The ride was bumpy. There were times when I held to the thin side-ropes of the toboggan for dear life. But we made good speed and covered ever so many more miles with it than we'd have been able to cover afoot during the several hours we were out. Parmelee, perched high in front, did all the driving—a wearisome job since the day was "all white." I sat on the toboggan, facing backward, with legs sticking out full length in the same direction. Stu knelt at the very end of the toboggan, facing me. Keeping to snow-covered parts of the valley floor, we headed westward toward Bracebridge Inlet.

Muskoxen,
Bathurst Island

Muskoxen,
Bathurst Island

When we were about two miles out of camp, Stu called my attention to a snowy owl overhead—an immaculate male bird, ghostlike against the white sky. All I could see at first were the big black beak and two slits of eyes floating a hundred feet above us. Excited by our approach—for we were close to his nest— he popped his mandibles loudly and repeated a harsh *quawk* as he swooped at us. Presently we hauled up at the nest. In it were seven nearly spherical white eggs, each but one bearing a red mark—evidence that an egg had been added to the clutch since Taylor's last visit. The nest was on a low mound in what would soon be marsh. The snow about the mound was several inches deep. A hundred yards away was the dark-green cloth blind that Taylor had been moving gradually closer. The female owl, whose plumage was heavily barred with dark gray, did not swoop at us. Standing on the ground a quarter of a mile off, she watched us calmly.

Our next stop was near a huge rock that Dave Parmelee had named the Sphinx —a recumbent monolith whose south end, viewed from the right angle, resembled a human profile. Contemplating this magnificent *tour de force* of wind, sun, frost, and time, I was reminded not so much of ancient Giza as of Jacob Epstein and Henry Moore; of the weirdly beautiful Easter Island heads; of arguments as to how a sincere abstraction differs from a cheap, essentially dishonest imitation of one; especially of inner musings as to why a statue—seen not from a fixed position, but as one moves past or around it—seems ever so gracefully to come to life.

By the time we had reached the head of the valley, the air had warmed considerably and the snow had become heavy and wet. Leaving the Ski-Doo, we

"... *viewed from the right angle, resembled a human profile.*"

"*The Sphinx," a huge rock that remained snow-free all winter along the north edge of the long valley west of the Bathurst camp. Photographed on 27 May 1968 by David F. Parmelee.*

walked southward up the gentle slope. MacDonald and Parmelee soon left me behind, for they needed to find as quickly as possible whether there was snow enough for crossing the ridge with the vehicle. While my friends were gone, I was escorted by five long-tailed jaegers whose insistence on staying near me was subtly flattering until I realized that they were after lemmings that my footfalls drove from the snow. There were lemmings aplenty. One that a jaeger caught not far from me kicked convulsively while the hooked beak whacked it against the ground.

"There's not enough snow here," announced Stu. "We'll have to go back a way. There's a chance of finding muskoxen almost anywhere this side of the big lake." Skirting the base of the ridge, we backtracked eastward, found a snow-filled gully, and started climbing. Where there was no snow, the Ski-Doo struggled noisily, but did not give up. To lighten the load, Stu and I got off. Reaching the top of the ridge at last, Parmelee left the vehicle in a patch of soggy snow. By this time he was a long way west of Stu and me.

I had to look twice to be sure I was right. On the slope just south of us, about a quarter of a mile away, were six dark spots—six muskoxen. One lifted its head and looked our way. As Parmelee approached from one direction, Stu and I from another, the animals drew together, though they did not form a circle. Following a little stream downslope, they looked at us occasionally, as if wondering whether their moving to another place were truly justifiable. Some purple sandpipers, feeding among the sedge, attracted our attention. A hen ptarmigan flew up, causing Stu to call out, for he was keen to locate as many pairs of these, his special birds, as possible. Not wholly forgetful of the muskoxen, we allowed ourselves to be distracted. When next we looked at them, they were forming a circle—a foregathering I had waited a lifetime to witness. How beautiful they were in their shaggy way, with their neat horns and stubby, white, knock-kneed forelegs! I studied them intently through my binocular. Something told me that I would be drawing a picture of them when I got back to camp.

Stu was pointing the hen ptarmigan out to me when suddenly the circle of muskoxen broke up. The animals facing us wheeled sharply as all six started on the run for the hill to the northeastward. For the next quarter of an hour the company was in view—so close together that they looked like a huge woolly-bear caterpillar undulating up the slope and away. What a sight it was! My excitement may well have amused my companions, who knew the ways of muskoxen well.

So "all-white" had the day been, hour after hour, that we'd hardly have noticed the snow that fell in early afternoon had it not clung to our eyelashes. In low country once more, headed back for camp, the Ski-Doo traveled rapidly, for here very little of the ground was bare. I hung on grimly. We came to a sudden stop. "Greater snow geese!" shouted Parmelee. "Right over there!"

I couldn't see the birds from my position on the sled; but when I got to my knees and trained my glass in the right direction, I saw them clearly—three pairs not far from each other, each bird orange-brown on the head and upper neck—an adventitious coloration that resulted from feeding and bathing in iron-impregnated water. One pair flew up alarmed, circled briefly, and alighted near the farthest pair, whereupon all six resumed feeding.

Dinner that night was especially good. Taylor gave us a report on his several

owl nests. His imitation of a male owl presenting a lemming to his mate; of the female's acceptance with lowered head wagging solemnly from side to side; of her standing straight, shaking out the long plumage of her underparts so as to expose the big bare brood-patch; and, finally, of her settling on the eggs with a smug, self-satisfied look on her face, was more than we could accept with decorum. We *yelled* applause. Our little friends the lemmings must have shivered in their tracks.

On June 15 winter returned. The north wind was strong and cold. Ground that had been muddy was as hard as rock. Ice covered every sheltered pool. I drew the circle of muskoxen from memory, then tackled a picture of two long-tailed jaegers flying. What I showed of landscape I drew directly from what I could see east of camp. The snow in the valley shone like satin, reflecting the sky. Most of the world was gray—gray sky, gray snow; but in the far distance were two intensely bright spots, one above Eastwind Point, one below—the latter so brilliant that it reminded me of a streetlight seen through frosted glass.

A discussion resulted from Taylor's announcement that at least one of his female owls had horns. This I could not accept. I had never seen a *horned* snowy owl in all my years of dealing with owls. What was more, I was unable to decide which head feathers *could* stand up enough to look like horns. Argument became heated and involved. The field sketches Taylor handed around certainly showed little horns, one above each eye. Might the wind produce these? Might Taylor be "seeing things?" Might the stiff feathers of the facial disc stand up in

"I was reminded not so much of ancient Giza
as of Jacob Epstein and Henry Moore;
of the weirdly beautiful Easter Island heads . . ."

Several huge monoliths north of Eeyore Hill
and east of North Star Rock were called "Stonehenge"
by the party that occupied the Bathurst camp in 1968.
Photographed on 28 May of that year by David F. Parmelee.

such a way as to look like horns? Taylor would not retract a word. Say what I might—and I said a good deal—that particular owl of his *had horns*.

The following day I was flabbergasted by Parmelee's report that at each of two owl nests visited by him the incubating bird had horns—little tufts that stuck up jauntily, that showed from the side, front, and back, and that waved in the wind. This was exasperating. I had to admit that my study of owls had never been from a blind; that I had never inspected a brooding owl through a binocular from afar; that my research had usually involved checking nests that were literally miles apart; that it had been chiefly a matter of protecting myself from attack rather than looking for details of plumage. I would see for myself. We would table the discussion.

There was excitement in camp when Parmelee mentioned two buff-breasted sandpipers he had seen in the low country. The buff-breast was not on the official bird list for Bathurst Island, so at least one specimen of the species was needed. Parmelee, Taylor, and I went after it. We scoured the snowless areas, fully realizing that protectively colored birds of this sort would be hard to see. Nowhere could we find one. Toward evening I went after one again, but in vain.

During my several hours of fieldwork that day I noticed that the snow seemed to melt more rapidly when the sun was under a cloud than it did when the sun was out—an observation that was counter to reason. I decided that when the air was warmed by the sun it started to rise, thus creating an updraft—and therefore wind—whose cooling effect retarded the snow's melting. Perhaps it was only an accident that I saw large trickles when the sun was hidden and small trickles when the sun came out. I should have forgotten buff-breasted sandpipers and been content with concentrating on one trickle.

Pierre Lamothe brought in a cock ptarmigan he had shot—a much needed specimen, for I wanted to base a painting on an unskinned bird with Stu's direct-from-life field sketch of the species' postcopulatory display in hand. The sketch showed the cock with vermilion combs lifted high, neck plumage puffed up, wings drooping, and tail lifted, spread to its greatest width, and tilted toward the crouching hen. Specimen in hand, I mapped the picture roughly to make certain that the central figures would stay within bounds yet not crowd each other. All went well until I came to the cock's tail with its sixteen feathers. These I could not seem to draw acceptably. Length would be right but foreshortening wrong, or perspective right but the feathers too close together and the tilt unconvincing. One sketch came so close to being correct that I shouted. Alas, when I counted the feathers, two were missing. Correcting this error required redrawing every feather except the middle pair. I did my best at holding the fanned tail with my left hand while plying pencil and eraser with my right, but this did not work. What I needed was a mounted specimen with tail in exactly the right position. Stu perceived my predicament, cut two narrow strips of cardboard, and pinned the spread rectrices so firmly between these that I could put the bird belly-down on the table, prop the fanned tail straight up, and pull tail, cardboard strips and all to one side and down with heavy thread into exactly the position needed.

Using this excellent though strange looking model, I forged ahead. When I had drawn and painted the tail—each feather glossy black except the middle

Greater
Snow Geese,
Bathurst Island

*Greater
Snow Geese,
Bathurst Island*

two—I showed the unfinished opus to Stu. "Magnificent" was his comment. "Magnificent!" he repeated. The crouching hen was a mere outline in pencil. The cock's lifted combs had received no vermilion. At lower left, below the cock's head, was a bit of willow, shown in great detail. Stu had called "magnificent" a drawing that was little more than started. In all seriousness I wondered whether what I had done might stand as greater "art" than the picture I intended to finish.

Part of each day I spent painting. Certain features of the scene that I saw through the windows became familiar, but as the season advanced there were striking changes. A steep slope just west of Eeyore Hill demanded attention for the snow there was pale brown, a color I could not account for until Phil Taylor explained that he has seen dust blowing down from eroded spots in the high country. I knew that under the lowest part of what lay north of us was the river. Presently this lowest part became a lovely pale blue—a promise that winter was ending.

On the evening of June 19 I went with Parmelee and MacDonald to the site of a blind from which they had made important observations at a sanderling nest the summer before. The circle of stones that had held the blind in place was conspicuous—for stones were hard to find in this country. Not far from the stones were two scrapes—neat, shallow cups in one of which the four precious eggs had been laid. In the blind four men, one at a time, had watched day after day, week after week, learning what it takes to bring sanderlings into the world.

"... neat, beautifully furred, perfectly toothed and clawed, equipped for a wonderful existence of their own."

A fully adult Collared Lemming in pepper-and-salt summer pelage out for a bit of sun not far from its burrow. Photographed by David F. Parmelee on 25 June 1969 about a mile west of the Bathurst camp.

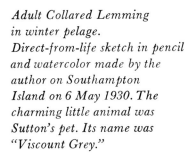

Adult Collared Lemming in winter pelage. Direct-from-life sketch in pencil and watercolor made by the author on Southampton Island on 6 May 1930. The charming little animal was Sutton's pet. Its name was "Viscount Grey."

There were moments of excitement when a jaeger, gull, or owl came close, but many long hours were uneventful. Stu will never forget the moment when, hearing a disturbance he could not explain, he stuck his head out to find himself face to face with a wolf. Stu's beard was heavy, iron-gray, and awesome; that beard and the glittering eyes must have given the wolf the surprise of its lifetime. Another high moment Stu described in excruciating detail. The time for hatching was at hand. Came sauntering by a baby hare—all innocence, all naiveté, wholly unaware of the dislike it was about to win for itself and for hares in general, when it hopped right into the nest, nicking an egg with its foot. The hare might as well have stabbed at Stu's heart. But MacDonald survived; the hare hopped on; *and the sanderling baby hatched!*

During an early morning walk on June 20 I saw scores of lemmings that the melt-water had driven from their burrows. In some areas, even on the very crest of the ridge, the mud was several inches deep and slithery. My bird list was considerably the largest for any day thus far: twenty or so long-tailed jaegers, two pomarine jaegers, one parasitic jaeger, one black-bellied plover, one purple sandpiper, and three or four red phalaropes. After breakfast I tried drawing a pair of phalaropes. The rich reddish brown of the female's plumage had a delicate purplish gray cast, almost a bloom, that I could not catch.

Parmelee's birthday came on June 20; but the celebration—meaning the cake —came the following day. This spicy, three-layered effusion was covered with thick chocolate icing held down by a three-dimensional snowy owl whose golden eyes were circlets of dried pear. Naturally this owl of owls had conspicuous horns; the discussion was untabled; and some of what was said was hot enough to scorch canvas.

But it was the wolves who stole the show that afternoon. I was working at a drawing of snow geese when Tuka made an odd noise and I looked out to see bent-over human forms pointing cameras toward the muskox remains south of the cook-tent. No one had cried *wolf*. No one had said anything that I could hear. But there the great creature was—long legged, lean faced, light buffy gray with dark saddle—a male Barren Grounds wolf, the first I had ever seen at close range. He was sniffing at the muskox bones. Occasionally he nibbled at a rib. I was tremendously impressed with his lankiness and with his masterful, dignified bearing. In a baffling, inexplicable way he did not seem wild. His glance was not furtive. His every move bespoke self-confidence. He had an odd way of pivoting on his hind feet and moving one front foot deliberately over the other as he looked around. The several human beings who were cautiously approaching did not seem to disturb him in the least. When he glanced straight at me I experienced an unexpected thrill—that "lean and hungry look" of his was *beautiful*. His eyes were not unfriendly. They demanded respect, but something about them bespoke wisdom and understanding.

His mate, a smaller, stockier animal than he, was nearly white. She did not linger in camp but moved out of sight down-slope and reappeared below the cook-tent running northward. For a moment I wondered whether there were three wolves rather than two. When the big male departed he ran slowly northwestward only a few rods from our Parcoll. I could see his head and the upper

part of his body for some time after his legs had disappeared below the highest part of the ridge. When finally every bit of him had passed out of sight I felt that I had seen a ghost. Despite the brightness of the sky behind him, his lanky form had cast no shadow.

I was the only man in camp most of Sunday, June 22. The snow covering the river was soggy and treacherous, yet MacDonald, Parmelee, and Taylor, on their way to high country beyond Hare Ridge, crossed without getting wet. At an owl nest they found one egg hatching and another starting to pip. Dave Gray and his assistant walked to the Laughing Rocks, where for a full half-hour they watched two cock ptarmigan in fierce combat. The rivals were so intent on victory that they paid little attention to the men. They were flying much of the time, chasing each other, but they rarely moved out of the circumscribed area each seemed to believe he was defending. To keep themselves upright when sparring on the ground, they partly opened their wings. Occasionally each took firm hold of the other's plumage with his beak and the two birds rolled over and over. An interesting fact their observers noted: the combatants lifted their feathers in such a way as to obscure the red combs above the eyes; had the birds been displaying before hens, these combs would have been conspicuous.

Parmelee found two greater snow goose nests on June 22—one with four eggs, the other with two. At each nest the goose was on the eggs and the gander on guard close by. At Parmelee's approach, each pair walked off. They did not fly.

Hour after hour that day I struggled with a phalarope drawing, but this second

"The muskox swung fiercely with his horns;
but the wolf—nimble, powerful, expert
—danced about, waiting for an opening."

"Old Bloodface," an adult male Barren Grounds Wolf,
approaching the carcass of a bull Muskox he has killed.
Photographed by David R. Gray on 28 May 1968 about five miles west
of Goodsir Inlet, Bathurst Island.
Photograph first appeared in the journal Arctic *in 1970 (Vol. 23, p. 146).*

attempt was no more successful than the first. Determined not to let failure depress me, I took a walk. This time I headed in a new direction, northeastward, and was surprised at the steepness of the slope a hundred yards beyond camp. Before and below me was the river—a long pool at the moment, with no perceptible current, the water beautifully clear. The submerged ice was pale green. Where the ice had melted, the sinister darkness of the bottom was visible.

In the flat country south of the river I happened upon a pair of oldsquaw ducks sunning themselves near a little pond. So comfortable were they, and so confiding, that they half shut their eyes when I stood quite still, even though I was only about twenty-five feet away. When I moved closer they stood up reluctantly, decided that something must be amiss, and waddled off. While I was watching them the sun went under a cloud and snow struck my face. The flakes settled lightly on the ducks. The thick, firm plumage kept the precious body heat from escaping, at the same time affording complete protection for the snow. The delicate flakes did not melt though they crumbled as the wind moved them. How Thoreau would have enjoyed those crystalline "sweepings from heaven's floor" as they eddied about on the ducks' broad backs!

Finally the hen flew up, followed closely by the drake. The pair circled widely and alighted along the far edge of the pond. The drake threw up his head and gave that musical, lustful, *ong, ong-a-way!* that I had enjoyed so many times, though never before at such close range.

That night the wind was fierce. The Parcoll shook violently. There was something contradictory and disquieting about being able to see so clearly the bellying and flapping of the hut's fabric, the shaking of the metal framework. Mac-

Donald's comment that the structure was guaranteed to withstand winds up to seventy miles per hour was not very reassuring. We all wondered what might be happening to the blind at Taylor's owl nest. When a box fell from the drying shelf hanging in the middle of the hut, I got up. A glance at the cook-tent was comforting; but the storm-porch at the front of the Parcoll lurched noisily and I thought for one terrifying moment that we were in for being blown—clothing, sleeping bags, cots, stovepipe and all—toward the biffy and the muskox carcass. No one uttered a syllable of complaint; but there was no badinage either.

Suddenly, shouted across the wind from the other Parcoll, muffled, but clear enough to make our four spines tingle, came the word *wolf!* The four "spines" hied themselves to windows, saw Old Bloodface at the muskox remains, hauled clothes on, pushed the roof of the storm-porch up enough to free the front door, and poured out into the gale. Old Bloodface had found something to gnaw at. He was in no hurry to leave. How superbly indifferent he was to the eight of us and to the fury of the wind! Experience must have taught him that human beings were not to be trusted; yet when he looked at me a certain twinkle of eye seemed to say: "Go ahead! Find a stick and throw it if you dare! You'd not hit me for one thing, and for another I just might fetch it for you!" A maudlin thought surely; a thought not entirely in good taste; and of course I never thought it . . . quite. Yet there the wolf was, not very far away, sedate, aloof, unafraid, at the point of accepting human beings as part of his habitat. Not as friends, quite. But not as foes either.

There he stood, thrilling me to the limits of my sensibilities, *prima-facie* evidence that part of the world was still wild, still unconquered, still not quite under

King Eiders,
Bathurst Island

King Eiders,
Bathurst Island

the human heel. Fascinated, I watched as the wolf gnawed a bit, lifted his head, turned to watch us, put his head down, and started gnawing again. Not once did he jerk as if from sudden misgivings. Not once did he bare his teeth or show the slightest animosity. When he left I was aware of a feeling close to grief. Perhaps I would never, never see a wild wolf again.

All day the savage wind continued. Even so, the redoubtable Parmelee struck out, determined to visit a spot at which he had banded a sanderling the summer before. While crossing the river on his way back to camp he broke through, caught his foot under thick ice, and found himself trapped. At the point of shooting three times as a signal for help, he took the shells from his shotgun, broke the ice by pounding downward with the gun's stock, and finally pulled free.

As for me, I worked hard at a wolf drawing. Never having drawn a wolf, I deeply regretted that my only model was the long-legged image that my mind held. Pierre and I were in charge of meals. In my diary appears this disgusting sentence: "The dish water was so laden with debris . . . it seemed a pity to throw it out."

On June 24 Dave Parmelee found a red phalarope's nest among dead grass in the marsh east of "the big lake." There were four eggs. This was the best evidence we had thus far come upon that summer had arrived. Phalaropes were *summer* birds. Half of the countryside was still under snow and most of the lake was ice-covered.

Conversation at meals so often centered on the importance of recording notes

fully and accurately, on the difference between conjectural and factual matter, on the painfully slow rate at which human knowledge accumulates, and on the many techniques used in illustrating articles and books on natural history, that we fell to calling ourselves "Bathurst Academy." Phil Taylor's life-size drawing of the head of a greater snow goose was excellent, though only an outline in pencil. Stu's tiny field sketches of ptarmigan were spirited and authentic. Dave Gray tried his hand at watercolor washes—first with a wolf drawing, then with a landscape showing East Wind Point. Pierre Lamothe amused us all by asking to borrow some of my cutouts of flying geese. "These could help me with some ideas I have had," he said. I was tempted to comment that with cutouts of mine he couldn't go wrong, but I held my peace.

I made a little watercolor sketch for each of the five younger men of the party. The one for Pierre was of two king eider drakes flying. Pierre was obviously touched by the gift. Holding it firmly to his chest he said: "This will always be close to me here, no matter where I go." Dave Gray made a handsome ring for me from a narrow cross-section of caribou antler. The "setting" was a little knob filed off in such a way as to produce a simple cameo. Not many people in this world are lucky enough to own a caribou cameo.

On June 25 Phil Taylor gave me a guided tour that I shall never forget. The weather was fine—so fine indeed that the brooks were breaking free. No one expected us to reach the nearest of the owl nests without getting wet. Equipped with a thin-handled pick, Phil led off merrily, reminding me that where the snow looked white and firm there was a chance of our getting to the middle of the valley dry. Each of us wore knee-high rubber boots.

Following the ridge westward, we occasionally crossed a streamlet big enough to be audible. About a mile from camp, a bit of bare ground blurred enough to

66

make us look twice. The blur was two running sanderlings close together about fifty feet ahead of us, one bird much more boldly marked than the other. "That bright bird's got a band on its leg!" shouted Phil, his voice louder than necessary. "That's got to be one of Dave Parmelee's birds!" We followed the pair for a quarter of an hour, but they did not lead us to a nest. "I'll have to go back and tell Dave right away," said Phil, as he stuck his pick in the ground not far from the spot at which we had first seen the birds.

I promised to keep track of the sanderlings as best I could. While Phil's form became steadily smaller, the nimble-footed pair led me all over the place, even across patches of snow. They made not the slightest effort, so far as I could see, to find food. Occasionally they paused to preen their plumage. Presently, after a short run upslope, they flew off westward over the horizon. I followed, but did not find them.

When Phil returned with Parmelee I reported my observations. The three of us walked rapidly in the direction the flying birds had taken and before long we found them. The pair were inseparable. They were on the move most of the time, running along about a foot apart, the female in the lead. Suddenly the female, facing into the wind, half-crouched as the male flew lightly to a point a few inches above her, descended slowly, and proceeded—with white-marked wings fluttering prettily, like a butterfly's—to do his part in making certain that the species sanderling would continue. Occasionally he grasped the feathers of his mate's head or neck with his bill. Not for an instant, during the approximately 148 seconds of copulation, did his wings cease to flutter.

Not far from the spot at which the mating had taken place, the female squatted, wriggled a bit, lifted her back plumage, and kicked vigorously. She was making or enlarging a "scrape." For one high moment we thought we had found the nest;

but presently she ran a few steps, paused to preen, and wandered aimlessly off with her mate.

Phil and I, eager to visit his owl nest, decided to leave Parmelee with the sanderlings. Pick in hand, my guide started downslope through snow about two feet deep. "Just stay where you are, Doc. Let me see how it goes," he called. "Maybe we'll have to try at another place." So I waited, while the considerate young man, now at the very foot of the ridge, made his way slowly, probing with his pick, occasionally steadied by it, step by step across the ominous stretch of whiteness below me. When I realized that Phil was *paving the way* for me, a much older man who had shown signs of falling apart, I straightened up; told myself to be ready to fall through, get wet, and come up grinning; and followed. Stepping precisely where Phil had stepped, a humiliating procedure that threw me off-balance occasionally, I caught up with him. With each new step he expected to go through; but no, the snow held, and presently we were out of it . . . on flat, wet ground two hundred yards from the nest and the dark-green blind.

I tried to express gratitude without admitting in so many words that I had needed help. Phil, to put me at ease, averred that he had gone to all that trouble only because he so hated getting himself wet. Oh, we were a polite twosome, each brimming with admiration—I for his youthful vigor and kindness, he for my philosophical, not to say hoary, outlook. "I can't wait to see the horns on that owl of yours," I said.

By the time we reached the nest the female owl had long since departed, but the eight eggs were warm. Not far from them lay two dead lemmings, each with a smear of blood where a claw had gone through the skin. The male owl did not attack us.

The dead lemmings affected me strangely. I could not be objective about them. There they lay, neat, beautifully furred, perfectly toothed and clawed, equipped for a wonderful existence of their own, but dead, stopped in their tracks, done for—all because they were an essential element in what we ecologists call a food chain. They were mature animals. Some of their progeny would live a while, reproducing like mad, making existence possible for snowy owls. They were the meek, the blesséd, dependable, expendable meek, inheritors of earth. As I looked down at them, questions that had bothered me as a youth bothered me once more. If the meek did indeed inherit the earth, then what did *inherit* mean? Keep things going? Make themselves fuel for the fire? Guarantee existence for others? Furnish bigger and better-heeled audiences for demagogues? Buy cosmetics by the ton to keep cosmeticians and advertising agencies prosperous? Ah me . . .

The blind was considerably the most elegant I had ever seen. Stu MacDonald himself had designed it. Seated on a box, I looked through a telescope trained on the nest, which was about 75 feet away. "Here's something for you," said Phil, handing me a candybar. "I'll leave you a while—half an hour, maybe. The owl will be back in no time when she sees me walking off." He pulled a zipper, shutting me in, and sloshed away.

The blind was wonderfully comfortable. My ungloved hands were warm. Out of the wind, my eyes functioned perfectly. *Why didn't someone tell me to bring my painting outfit?* I muttered to myself. *Someone should have explained how comfortable this would be! Why . . .* The thought never got finished, for there the great owl was, golden eyes wide open, black beak parted, wings full-spread, letting herself down to the nest. Having alighted, she glared for two or three long

"There was nothing imaginary about them."

*Female Snowy Owl on nest in the Goodsir valley west
of the Bathurst camp. The feather "horns" that show plainly here
were a storm-center of discussion for a week or so.
Photographed by David F. Parmelee on 21 June 1969.*

seconds at the blind, then looked northward at her mate, who was flying grandly about with neck outstretched and wings beating slowly. What she saw must have met with her approval, for she lowered her head, pushed her eggs about with her beak, lifted her long, soft belly plumage and proceeded so convincingly with all that Phil had imitated in his after-dinner act that the scientist within me was hard put staying in command. After wriggling down into a comfortable position on her eggs, her back plumage sank, her eyes slowly narrowed, and above each eye appeared . . . *a neat little triangular horn!*

I saw a good deal of those horns. There was nothing imaginary about them. They were visible even when the bird faced away from me, for then, being in shadow, they became very dark. They waved in the wind. Only when the owl became excited enough to lift her head or stand up did they vanish. Let her become composed, narrow-eyed, and sleepy-looking and lo, there the horns were again!

Accidentally I moved the telescope a trifle and the owl took alarm, stood up, and made off swiftly. I watched her alight, two hundred yards away. Her mate appeared, swooped at her, making her crouch, then circled with wings beating so slowly that the forepart of his body sank perceptibly at the end of each down-stroke.

I had more than the owls to watch, for a company of five caribou, each with stubby, partly grown antlers, appeared on the bare slope beyond the snow at the valley's edge. Seeking provender, heads down much of the time, they moved along hurriedly, as if late for an appointment. I hoped they would come close, but they stayed on the slope, making their way toward Eeyore Hill.

71

*Greater
Snow Geese,
Bathurst Island*

the important first egg was there—stone cold. No bird of either sex was in evidence. Parmelee waited, waited, waited, hour after hour. At last, slipping in like a little ghost, the hen sanderling came, deposited her second egg, and made off. In Parmelee's mind a strange idea had been gaining strength: perhaps a female sanderling normally lays *two* clutches at the beginning of the reproductive cycle, each clutch of four eggs, one clutch for her mate, one for herself. Such a procedure would explain contradictory published statements to the effect that only the female or only the male attended the eggs. But how would the eggs be deposited—the first in the male's scrape, the second in the female's, the third in the male's, and so on? Or would all four eggs of the male's clutch be laid before the female's clutch was started? How far apart would the two nests be? Above all, how much coldness could a fresh egg endure? Presumably no egg would receive incubation before the clutch was complete—a procedure insuring simultaneity of hatching, of departure of the brood from the nest, and of fledging. Might a kind of rest period during which the germ-cell was subjected to many hours of coldness somehow *benefit* the developing embryo? Answering questions such as these would require a great deal of work during the egg-laying period: finding the two scrapes; recording air temperature at ground-level around the clock; color-marking the two adult birds in such a way as to make individual recognition easy; and observing the marked birds continuously until each had settled down to steady incubation.

When Parmelee witnessed the laying of the second egg in that particular scrape he felt reasonably sure that a full clutch is laid in one scrape before another clutch is started. This much he felt that he *knew*, for he had watched the female

*"... four men, one at a time, had watched day
after day, week after week, learning what it takes
to bring sanderlings into the world."*

*Male Sanderling incubating eggs. Photographed not far from
the Bathurst camp by David F. Parmelee.
Photograph first appeared in* The Living Bird, *the annual
of the Laboratory of Ornithology at Cornell University, in 1970.*

bird working at that very scrape the day before; he had observed the empty scrape after the female had left it; and he had seen the one egg in it a few hours later. But now that two eggs were in it, he fell to wondering about the male bird. Might the male be incubating a full clutch at another nest? All Parmelee could do was wonder, for the male bird was nowhere to be seen.

Stu MacDonald decided that a pair of greater snow geese should be obtained for the museum. He collected a pair that had a nest along the edge of the valley below Skull Rise. The gander weighed 6¾ pounds, the mate a pound less. So beautiful was the gander's purplish pink bill with its ivory-colored "nail" at the front, its black side-markings or "grinning patches," and its neat rows of "teeth," that I set to work at once painting the head before the colors of the fleshy parts had had a chance to fade. The drawing demanded close attention for about three hours.

Needing a break, I changed to field garb and headed southwestward from camp. I wanted to see for myself a tarn along whose edge red-throated loons had nested the preceding summer. The walking was sometimes difficult, for parts of the ridgetop were so muddy that I sank in badly. Two miles from camp I began wondering whether I had taken the wrong direction. Bewildered, I climbed a smooth-topped eminence and there, surrounded by snow and not far away, though at considerably lower level, lay the tarn, its steel-blue surface wrinkled by the wind. Clouds above the northern horizon were lead-gray. Patches of open sky overhead were bright azure. Why, then, the steel-blue? I was not enough of a physicist to explain that dark, cold-looking, startingly beautiful color.

Between me and the tarn lay a neat mosaic of polygons—a by-product of frost action. Here and there a mossy spot hinted of green. Listening carefully, I heard the murmur of water running and the distant squealing of jaegers. On a page in my pocket notebook I sketched what I saw—a steel-blue sapphire, as it were, resting on a triangular altar-cloth of white satin.

The following morning I put the little sketch to work. The painting was of two greater snow geese, with the tarn in the background. I worked away happily, alone in the Parcoll. Parmelee was blowing eggs in the cook-tent; Stu and Phil were skinning geese outdoors, in a sheltered spot somewhere; and the other four men were afield. I finished the painting that day.

On June 28 we had delicious greater snow goose omelet for breakfast. A hearty meal was in order since Parmelee, convinced that there should be a sanderling nest near a spot at which he had caught and banded a male sanderling at its nest the summer before, had persuaded Stu to accompany him on a nest-finding foray. The spot Dave had in mind was several miles north of camp. Equipment included a great coil of heavy rope.

Planning their operation so as to cover the ground thoroughly, the two men marched back and forth, back and forth, dragging the rope between them in such a way as to flush the sanderling from its eggs. Whether the bird would prove to be the male or the female was beside the point. Finding the nest was the job to be done. All went well enough for three hours or so, save that no bird flew up. A band of muskoxen, feeding close by, continued to be something of a problem. Instead of forming a circle or running off, the animals remained in the area,

Sanderling

glancing at the men occasionally, but obviously unalarmed. Parmelee feared that one of the great beasts would step on the nest. The rope-draggers, by this time of divided mind, for they could not help wondering what the muskoxen might do next, went on with their work. Tired, all but convinced that further effort would be futile, they were about to call it a day when Parmelee shouted: "Let's try once more! One more drag, right where that muskox was!" They dragged, this time fairly certain that the muskox would cause trouble, and up the sanderling flew!

Excitement knew no bounds. The muskox could have gored and trampled the two of them and the two would have come up laughing. The four eggs were beautiful—a fact no doubt proclaimed by Parmelee, whose eyes no doubt were shining. But the most amazing discovery of all was that the incubating bird was a *banded* male. It was the very male that Parmelee had banded at a nest in that area the year before. So devoted was the bird to its eggs that it refused to leave them. Stu caught it in his hand. This was ornithological history in the making.

When the two men came in, rope and all, I could tell that they had worked hard. But they were happy. They handed me the perfect sanderling, one that I knew I'd have to paint at once, despite the lateness of the hour. I examined the metal band, spread the wings, counted the three slender, webless toes on each foot. How *little* the bird was! How far had it travelled since the day on which it had been banded? What gales had it weathered, what oceans crossed? As its portraitist-to-be I despaired of capturing the lovely *frosted* look of its head, neck, and chest plumage—an effect produced by the grayish white tipping on the cinnamon-colored feathers. Groaning inwardly, I tackled the drawing. I knew what to expect

*"Who could bring himself to kill a muskox,
to end a life won against such incredible odds?"*

*David F. Parmelee and a "mean" bull Muskox into which
David R. Gray tried—with small success—to fire tranquilizer darts.
Seen through the wonderfully clear arctic atmosphere,
the Muskox appears to be much smaller than it actually is.
In the far distance is one of the "Laughing Heads."
Photographed by Philip Taylor not far from our Bathurst camp.*

of the tough paper; I could erase to my heart's content. I knew enough to sharpen the pencil well. The light was good. The brushes were dependable. A large brush with fine tip helped with the intricate patterns. The picture turned out well.

Dinner that evening was late and sumptuous—spring goose. I continued to be amazed by Stu's ability as *chef de cuisine*. Conversation centered in the long-planned-for flight that would take Stu, Dave Parmelee, Phil, and me northward first to Eureka, on Ellesmere Island, then across Axel Heiberg Island to Meighen Island. Eureka was "home" for Stu and Dave, who had spent several months there in 1955. As for Meighen, the lure was ivory gulls. Someone had reported seeing pure white gulls in that part of the Canadian Arctic Archipelago and it was obvious that one David F. Parmelee would know no peace until he had discovered at least one ivory gull's nest there. "Just look at those eggs! Did you ever see anything so beautiful?" I could hear him saying. Whereupon I would fall to wondering how many ivory gull nests could be expected to hold more than one egg.

The possibility that summer was already on the wane perturbed us. A considerable stretch of the Goodsir River was now open directly north of camp. Saxifrage was blooming on every southward-facing slope. Unless we got to the ivory gulls soon we'd be finding downy chicks instead of eggs. The Otter that would take us to Eureka and to Meighen was at Resolute. Messages that flew back and forth via Devon Island informed us that weather conditions were bad at Resolute; that we need not expect the Otter until safe departure from Resolute and safe arrival at Bathurst were assured.

On June 29 we were in a wretched tizzy. No one dared go afield for fear the Otter would suddenly appear. The weather was fine, the confusion so much the worse. Dave Parmelee hated leaving his precious sanderling eggs, Phil Taylor his owls. My chief trouble lay in my inability to figure out what the plan was. The more I questioned Stu, the more fully I realized that even he was in doubt as to how things would go. Would we fly straight to Eureka, then back to Bathurst? Would we camp on Meighen? What gear would I myself truly need? I decided that further painting was out of the question; that every bit of extra clothing—boots, socks, underwear, what not—should be left with the lads at Bathurst Academy on the Goodsir.

It all worked out nicely. On the last day of June, Harold Mordy flew in with his Otter and alighted without incident. We packed everything—including Tuka, who had been ailing—and said goodbye. Departure was a short run first on level ground, then sharply downward on the slope north of camp, and takeoff just short of the river's edge. I hated myself for being so frightened, but frightened I was. I had never experienced a takeoff anything like that. We flew not to Eureka, but back to Resolute.

Waiting at Resolute for safe flying weather can try patience sorely, bring out the devil in one's nature, and use up traveller's checks at an alarming rate. This time we were lucky. On July 1 Harold Mordy informed us that word from Eureka was encouraging and that he and his Otter were ready, so off we went.

The several-hundred-mile flight to Eureka was an experience in resignation. For me all flying is that, to some extent, for I know nothing of operating aircraft; but there is something about the arctic scene—as viewed from a comfortable

86

plane—that demands a curbing of the imagination, a refusal to worry, and an humble acknowledgement of one's dependence on machine and pilot. Nowhere below is there a sign of road or human habitation. Nowhere in all this vast expanse of rock and sea is there a town, a trading post, or even an Eskimo village. The thought is frightening. Therefore do not think; steer away from thought; give thought wide berth. Loosen the spine. Play the sybarite for the nonce. Sit back limply, uselessly, glorying in mankind's ability to move above, to look down upon, to contemplate the mile upon mile, mile upon mile of barren rock; the white lace woven of snow-filled cracks, seams, and gorges; sheer cliffs that tower thousands of feet above the frozen sea; the blue-green of ocean ice with its neat cracks, many of them remarkably straight; the blackness of open water at narrow "leads" along the shore. Enjoy for its softness the cloud that hides the cliff. Pick out the ledge on which gyrfalcons or peregrines might nest. Search eagerly for the splotch of whitewash marking the eyrie and rejoice in the fact that there is no hazardous descent with rope in store for you. Look for seals; they like to bask in the sun near the cracks. Look for orange-colored cliffs—cliffs where the droppings of seabirds have furnished enough nitrogenous material to make life for a forest of lichen possible. Look for the seabirds themselves—kittiwake gulls, perhaps. They are so far below the plane that they are almost imperceptible; but once sighted they sparkle and glitter, reminding one of goldstone or of childhood's glass paperweight with its tiny white floating particles.

Eureka is fully five degrees of latitude farther north than Resolute. What we flew over in getting there looked wintry indeed, for very little of the ocean was open; we were much too far above ground to see such evidence of summer as

87

flowers; and there was much snow on the shadowed side of steep ridges. I recall wondering again and again where we were. The land-mass just north of Resolute was, of course, Cornwallis Island. According to the map, Maury Channel and Baillie-Hamilton Island were directly north of Cornwallis Island, but we must have flown east of these. What part of the ocean was below us? Was it the northern end of Wellington Channel, and could that channel have been named for the duke who conquered Napoleon at Waterloo? Overcome by a strange mixture of torpor and ecstasy I decided to let the lands and waters down there go unidentified. Somewhere there'd be a Devon Island, with its huge Grinnell Peninsula, somewhere a Graham Island and a Norwegian Bay. "That's Axel Heiberg," came Dave's voice above the roar of the propellers, and I looked down on dark basaltic pinnacles and spires so close and gliding by so fast that they, not we, seemed to be moving—dancing a slow pavan, as it were, with their robe-covered feet on the glaucous green glassy floor.

Long before seeing the station buildings, Stu and Dave recognized Eureka Sound, Slidre Fjord, the Sawtooth Range, Blacktop Ridge, and a hill they called the Falcon's Castle. In great excitement they pointed these features out, at the same time calling attention to the fact that there was almost no snow anywhere in the low country; that the north side of the fjord was free of ice; and that the delicate purple shimmer on the slopes was saxifrage in full bloom. We had reached a surprisingly mild, a somehow benign part of the arctic, a sort of Promised Land. It was almost as if we had travelled *south*. I noticed the difference the minute I stepped out of the plane. The wind was strong enough; it certainly was not balmy; but it had no teeth. Stu and Dave were wonderfully jovial; every

part of our surroundings roused memories for them—of strenuous climbs up Blacktop; of families of wolves; especially of an awkward wolf cub they had caught and carried to camp in their arms while the mother wolf—obviously concerned, but not in the least savage—had trotted along a few paces to one side of them.

At the station itself—a good half-mile from the landing strip—there was an aggregation of long-tailed jaegers larger than any I had ever seen—literally scores of the graceful pirates, waiting for a handout. The men had been feeding them, of course. The birds were embarrassingly companionable—like cats stroking legs in hopes of receiving cream. Wheeling, dipping, hovering, occasionally squealing, they watched every man, every window, every door. Especially did they watch every hand, for it was from hands that the pieces of bread came. Often they caught a piece in midair. How bright their eyes were! What fun it was to hear their wings rustle, to watch them suddenly let down their legs and spread their webbed toes wide, putting on brakes! I counted over sixty at one time, most of them in the air.

Word reached us that weather conditions were favorable at Meighen Island so, after a sketchy meal, off we flew again, this time due westward. The wild, jagged beauty of Axel Heiberg as we saw it that day—the blackness of its rock, more than half hidden by snow and ice, and the whiteness of the low-flying clouds, I shall long remember. The curved foot of one glacier was so symmetrical, so nearly semicircular, that I was awed. The white mass, debouching from a high canyon, reminded me of a huge frosted fig, pressed flat though not quite to the bursting point, its stem hidden back of a pinnacle, its opposite, fanned-out end not far above sea level. I continued to hope that we would see a raven or a gyrfalcon, but not a bird did we see. Most of the slopes were far too steep and barren for caribou or muskoxen.

Meighen was a wholly different sort of island. We did not see all of it, of course, but what we did see was comparatively flat. I recall wondering, as we flew low over its northern coast, whether we were coming in for a landing. Below us was the meteorologists' camp I had heard of, and those moving objects were human beings, creatures of our species, waving their arms. We dropped mail but did not alight. There was no need for visiting the camp, since all was well there. What was more to the point, we were not much interested in Meighen. The place we wanted to see was Perley.

Perley had been described for me as an island—a small, flat island over which someone had seen at least one pure white gull flying. A map that I had inspected had shown Perley as a bit of land just north of Meighen. But what we saw on that first day of July, 1969, as Harold Mordy flew the Otter within inches of what land there was, convinced me that Perley was neither island nor islet but archipelago. The statement sounds flippant, but I offer it seriously. It may be one island at high tide, many islands at low: that is possible. In any event, we scoured Perley thoroughly—back and forth, round and round, often so close to the ground, water or ice that I sat there in lockjawed misery until the blessed thought entered my mind that Harold Mordy probably valued his own life more than he did ours; that he knew his Otter well; that, in an important sense of the clause, he and the Otter were one.

Perley was not beautiful. What we saw of it was incredibly flat, much of it

*Oldsquaw
drake,
Bathurst Island*

*Oldsquaw
drake,
Bathurst Island*

under shallow water or rotting ice. I looked in vain for vegetation. Phil Taylor thought he saw a gull or two, but he could not be sure that they were pure white. We flew back to Eureka, comforted as we looked down on Axel Heiberg, realizing that the cliffs below us were much too far away for scraping.

The station at Eureka was not far from the shore of the fjord, near the mouth of a shallow brook. Beyond the brook was rolling country in which Stu, Dave, and Phil planned to record the flightsongs of knots. Attracted to the gentle slope between the landing strip and Blacktop Ridge, I decided to go that way by myself, taking a binocular but no gun. I had been sitting still for hours, so needed a walk.

On the road to the landing strip I was all but overwhelmed by three big huskies who were obviously just as eager to stretch their legs as I. They boiled around my feet, impeding every step. At my yelled "Stay home!" and waved arms they bounced off gleefully, only to bounce back again. I started to pick up a rock and the largest tried to get the rock for me, gave my neck a noisy lick while I was leaning over, and punched me so hard with his nose that I almost buckled. When I straightened up, he gave my right hand an oddly affectionate nuzzle that seemed to say, "Think nothing of it. You know I meant well." Not for the life of me could I comprehend why the dogs were so eager to go along. They had all the time any dog could want, now that it was summer. The whole outdoors was theirs. It must have been the companionship that they craved—the joy of sharing with another mortal the bright sky, the wind, and the spicy fragrance of the tiny, white arctic heather bells.

By the time I reached the landing strip, the huskies were no longer bothersome. Indeed, they had scattered a bit. The serious-minded one had gone ahead. One had stayed behind, limping a little. The biggest was a rod or so to one side, eager to come closer if I gave him the slightest encouragement. Snow buntings that had a nest or young ones on the far side of a gully attracted my attention. I sat on a rock, watching the birds through my binocular. Somewhat to my relief, the huskies went on. I was tempted to call them back, especially the big bruiser whom I'd grown to like, but I let them go. Smaller, ever smaller they became, looking like "toy" huskies as they climbed a shoulder of the slope far to my right, and disappeared. How uneventful life promised to be without them!

I had no desire to climb Blacktop, but I did want to reach ground high enough to permit me to look down on station, fjord, and landing strip all at one time. Knowing that sooner or later I'd have to cross the gully that led up to the foot of the ridge proper, I chose a gentle declivity and picked my way to the bottom. Walking was tricky, for the spongy hummocks were so far apart that each step required a look, a push with one foot, and a sort of reaching out and grabbing with the other. The stream bed was dry. On higher land at last, I surveyed the slopes below me, failing for a time to notice a band of muskoxen, all at rest, on flat ground at slightly higher level several hundred yards away. Most of the nine animals appeared to be fully adult, but one was somewhat undersized, a yearling perhaps, and one a very young calf.

The calf greatly interested me. I recalled that at Bathurst we had discussed the failure of reproduction among muskoxen there. Calves were born toward the end of winter, yet David Gray had not found a single calf on Bathurst in 1969. I remembered, too, a charming picture Dave Parmelee had shown me of a calf— a photograph taken on Axel Heiberg. Accidentally separated from its mother,

who had raced off with the herd when frightened by a snow vehicle, the calf had persisted in punching Dave and his companions back of the knees in its attempts to find nourishment.

While I was looking the muskoxen over, one by one, through the binocular, a gray-white dog, obviously not one of the three that had accompanied me, ran upslope toward the muskoxen, causing them to rise abruptly and form a circle. Now I could not see the calf at all. The head of every animal was lowered, ready for battle.

My reaction was unpleasant. Suddenly I felt responsible and guilty. The dogs probably had come along with me against station rules. That was the reason for their being so gleeful! Now there'd be trouble. Either a muskox would be hurt or at least one dog would be hurt or killed and I'd be to blame. I should have made clear that I was going for a walk and that it was not my wish nor my intention to take the dogs along. I was much too far away to try calling the gray-white dog back. Furthermore, I knew that the gray-white dog would pay no more attention to me than the other three had. Oh well, I told myself, as I headed back for the station—hoping against hope that all the dogs would follow —those huskies must surely have chased muskoxen around here before, and the muskoxen must surely have learned how to deal with them. There was justification for this thinking, for the gray-white dog, tired of running around the horned circle, was now trotting off, and the circle had broken up. I could see the calf once more—a tiny thing, slightly darker than the older animals.

An hour later, back at the station, my first question was: "How many dogs do you have here?" The answer: "Three. They all went with you. They love to get out, you know. One of them hates everybody. He got a good beating a while back, and he's never forgotten it; but he goes along anyway." My gray-white "dog" had been a wolf, a wild Barren Grounds wolf—something I should have known, for its tail had not curled, husky-fashion, up over its back.

Late that evening, in a windless spot near one of the buildings, I happened upon a company of about thirty long-tailed jaegers, most of them sound asleep. The almost horizontal rays of the sun gave their creamy white breasts an aureate brilliance that was hard to believe. The birds that were awake may have looked at me twice, to make sure that I had no food for them, but they showed no sign of walking off or of spreading their wings, though I approached to within twenty feet. As if to remind me of the hour, the nearest one yawned—right in my face!

Sleeping that night was so sound and emerging from the sleeping bag so painless the following morning that what I heard from Stu, Dave, and Phil about their observations of displaying knots seemed part of a pleasant dream. The dream continued as I ate breakfast, listened to comments on the brightness of the weather, and heard Harold Mordy say that a flight to the Falcon's Castle would be possible. The dream continued as we were driven to the landing strip; it continued while pilot and assistant discussed plans. It continued . . .

Abruptly it ended when a tensing of neck muscles informed me that what we were looking at—less than a hundred yards away—was not something imagined, not an apparition, but *three white wolves.* Someone had said "wolves," to be sure. I had heard the word. But that had been part of the dream. The thought that something might be genuinely wrong with me unless I quit seeing an *apparition* and started thinking *wolves,* wakened me thoroughly. They were living

animals, those three—real wolves, an adult male, an adult female, and an almost full-grown cub. They were white, but not by any means snow-white. Their fur had a soiled, slightly moth-eaten look. They probably had been running, for their mouths were open and their tongues hanging out. The slight upcurling of their lips put a grin on their faces. They took off downslope, pausing to look back now and then, not really afraid, but in doubt and curious.

Curious indeed was one of them—the big male—for all at once there he was again, closer than ever, and moving closer. What he had seen or smelled had been too much for him, so back he had come for more. Parmelee, camera in hand, walked slowly toward him and kneeled. The wolf, more curious than ever, came closer. I could not keep the time-honored word *ravening* from mind. Could this wolf be real? Might this show of curiosity be a tactic? Might our friend Dave be in danger? These were completely honest thoughts that came and went. The wolf, stiff-legged, not quite sure of himself, tense, as if ready for trouble, drew a bit closer, looked earnestly at Dave and his camera, glanced in our direction, and also went.

For years I had been hearing about the Falcon's Castle—a sandstone eminence on which a pair of white gyrfalcons had had their eyrie in the spring of 1955. We had seen the "castle" as we had flown in, but I was keen for a closer look. Especially did I want to see a gyrfalcon.

The Otter carried us southward across the fjord, heading straight for a buffy yellow ridge whose very top reminded me of the fossilized, still partly buried spine of a huge prehistoric reptile. Wind and frost had eroded the slopes away, leaving grotesque remains. Nowhere was there an awe-inspiring cliff, but the

*"... hopped from one clump of saxifrage to another,
nipping flowers off with its sharp incisors."*

*A somewhat brown-eared, brown-nosed Arctic Hare in full summer pelage
photographed by David F. Parmelee on 3 July 1968
on a bluff about three miles north of the Bathurst camp.*

whole ridge-top looked decrepit, rotten, ready to disintegrate. Round and round it we flew, noting that the sand fanning out from its base was utterly without vegetation. Alas, we saw no gyrfalcon.

What we did see, not on the "castle" itself nor on the sand at its base, but all over the rest of the ridge, were arctic hares—fluffy white creatures bigger than jack rabbits. Nowhere had I seen hares so large or in such abundance. I counted seven in one company, sixteen in another, over twenty in another. They gave parts of the terrain a sort of polka dot effect. I hoped one would stand up, flailing the air with its paws, or hop along on its hind feet, but they all stayed low, dozing in the sun or moving casually about, seeking provender. I was struck with the fact that they kept their ears down most of the time. They were not in the least protectively colored now that the snow had melted.

Failure of these hares to turn dark in summer would have been confusing had I not mulled over certain facts—the most important of these being that Eureka's latitude was high. The 75th parallel ran "right through the station," I had been told. At such high latitudes summer was exceedingly short, winter correspondingly long. Had the hares been obliged to molt out of a white winter pelage into a dark one, then, within six weeks or so, back into a white one, the draining off of energy would have been considerable, possibly detrimental. The whole congeries of basal metabolism; of thermoregulation during a season likely to be extremely variable weatherwise; of the blood's work of carrying melanin granules to the developing dark hairs—all this was involved. White the hares remained all year—the continuing existence of their species being proof enough that the disadvantages of whiteness in summer were somehow outweighed by the advantages. In the back of my mind lurked a suspicion that nature *could* have found a way of making the two rapid-fire molts safe even at a high latitude; but skipping one molt was probably simpler. What I was thinking applied, of course, to adult animals. Young hares at Eureka were gray during their first summer.

There must have been a reason for the extraordinary local abundance of hares near the Falcon's Castle. Food must have been plentiful there. Vegetation covered about a fifth of the ground, much of it saxifrage, a favorite hare food. Such plants as avens, groundsel, sour-dock, bladder campion, and lousewort—not to mention grasses, sedges, and lichens—probably were there too. But what about willow? I suddenly realized that below Blacktop Ridge I had seen both musk-oxen and willow *but not a single hare.* Here there were hares galore but precious little willow and no muskoxen. Could the vegetal sum-total of an area determine the distribution of certain mammals to this extent? Absence of hares from an area on one summer day and abundance of hares in a not-very-far-removed area on the very next day struck me as being more than accidental.

I needed answers to several questions. Did all these hares live near the Falcon's Castle all summer long? I had read of the great herds of hares seen by explorers at high northern latitudes in winter. Dave Parmelee himself had told me of veritable roadways of tracks made by roving bands in the snow. I had assumed that when the breeding season arrived these bands would break up into scattered pairs. If the slopes surrounding the Falcon's Castle were indeed the hares' summer home, where were the gray young ones? Could this entire population have failed to reproduce? Could all the gray young ones have been captured by predators?

102

Rock Ptarmigan

I pondered the possibility that the young ones had been there, invisible because of their grayness, or old enough to be largely white. I wondered whether what we saw was the entire Eureka population foregathered at that one spot because of the abundance of favorite food-plants. The thought crossed my mind that all these hares *might* come together for an intensive feeding period once or twice a day, and scatter widely when finished with feeding. One question above all others bothered me, as it had for years. What preyed regularly on adult hares? Wolves preyed on muskoxen, thus supplying themselves with food and at the same time preventing overabundance of muskoxen. What factor or factors continued to cut the hare population down to size?

The question was not silly. Those hares were fully as large as the largest arctic fox I had ever seen. They were considerably larger than hares I had seen on Southampton and Baffin islands. Stu MacDonald had told me that adult hares handled by him at Eureka had weighed 10 to 12 pounds, whereas adult foxes there had averaged 6½ to 7 pounds. Almost certainly arctic foxes did not prey on adult hares at all regularly on Ellesmere Island. So long as muskoxen and caribou were plentiful, wolves probably paid little attention to hares. Surely the teeth of weasels were not long enough to get through an adult hare's thick fur to some vital spot. I recalled Stu MacDonald's vivid account of a snowy owl's attempts to capture an adult hare. The owl swooped repeatedly and the hare, instead of running off, remained stock still until the owl was very close, then jumped like a flash to one side, moving only a short distance, but completely outmaneuvering the owl. Crowding my mind was a suspicion that the hares at Eureka were over-abundant—this despite the fact that they all looked healthy.

The life of their species, *Lepus arcticus,* might very well be cyclic, like that of their more southern relative, the varying hare, *Lepus americanus.* Had the Eureka population been steadily increasing—working toward food-shortage, starvation, and disease—a syndrome preceding crash? More than once I had observed dramatic abundance of lemmings in the far north. Never before had I observed such spectacular abundance of hares. The phenomenon was impressive and thought-provoking.

Leaving the Falcon's Castle without alighting, the Otter took us to East Wind Lake, where MacDonald and Parmelee had had a camp in 1955. The low land surrounding the lake and the smooth slopes leading up to Blacktop were the most verdant I had seen in weeks, though nowhere were they really green. The vegetation was short and ground-hugging. With my binocular I made out virescent spots that might have been stands of equisetum; yellow that could have been the petals of poppies; red that could have been the stalks of oxalis or "sour-grass." The very special beauty of arctic vegetation could never, I knew, be seen from the air. To see it well, indeed to see it at all, one should be walking or, better still, kneeling.

A company of muskoxen were obviously perplexed by the Otter, for they stood quite still, watching us. When we headed in their direction they started running—upslope, downslope, obviously bewildered. For a time they moved like a single organism, all turning now this way, now that, reminding me of a flock of flying shorebirds; but suddenly they split up, some going one way, some another, plus one animal of divided allegiance—caught, as it were, by indecision—all at once highly vulnerable, apart from the others. It was individuals of this category, I

*". . . carried away by the statuesque beauty
of the animal itself."*

*A bull Peary's Caribou with antlers "in the velvet."
Photographed by David F. Parmelee on 24 July 1968 in the wide
Goodsir valley about a mile northwest of the Bathurst camp.*

could not help thinking, that were cut down by the wolves.

Not far from the lake the Otter attempted to alight, but the ground was too rough or too muddy and up we roared with an immediacy that left my stomach behind. The whole experience—realization that we might alight, that we were slowing down; a muffled sound somewhere; a slight bump that might have been a signal from landing gear to pilot; and the unexpected, almost explosive, return to the sky—all this had been so swift, so utterly beyond my control, that I had to fight for equanimity. A glance at the distant muskoxen helped. There they were, blissfully reunited, close together but not obviously on the defensive, safe in their blessed habitat, with their feet on the blessed ground.

Those remarkable animals! All the way back to the station I thought about them, marvelling once more over the simple fact of their being where they were at the moment and over the far less simple fact of my having been there to see them. Why did I feel so deeply about them? Was it because they embodied in some special way that which I had come to love about the far north? Was it because they had revealed an important part of myself to me and in so doing had *become* part of me? Questions of this sort I could not answer. What I could do—and this I felt very deeply—was oppose with all my might the killing of muskoxen as "game." Biologists employed by conservation departments might argue that a few muskoxen could be spared. Politicians with an eye on the vote might insist that an open season would be "good business" for airlines and bush pilots, for northern hostelries, even for the government, if a thousand dollar license fee were charged. But who could bring himself to kill a muskox, to end a life won against such incredible odds?

At the station I watched a male snow bunting for a quarter of an hour. The sparrow-sized black-and-white bird spent most of its time jumping for seeds that it jerked free from stems five or six inches up. Not once did it open its wings while jumping.

On our way back to Resolute we stopped for several hours at the high southern end of Baillie-Hamilton Island. Dave and Stu wanted to re-visit a large kittiwake gullery there—certainly among the northernmost kittiwake colonies in the world. The Otter alighted without trouble; Stu, Dave, Phil, and I promised to return "right off" if the weather worsened; and the four of us headed southwestward. What we could see of the ocean from the island's top was sealed shut with ice; but as we moved downslope we perceived that the stretch of open water along the shore was much more than a lead; it was a kind of lake.

A quarter of a mile from the plane we came upon a bull caribou whose antlers, though still in the velvet, were magnificent. The animal was standing quite still, watching us calmly. "What a picture!" I said aloud, carried away by the statuesque beauty of the animal itself—so still, so utterly motionless—and of the wind-struck water, pale grey ocean ice, and fog-hung horizon behind it. As if to overcome apprehension, the caribou took a few steps, tossed his head, looked our way again, and returned to filling up on saxifrage. I noticed that he did not pull up whole plants. He took a nip here, a nip there, as he moved along, following what was probably a time-honored custom that assured a continuing food supply for great numbers of caribou. Presently he must have sensed that something was wrong, for he lifted his nose high—a movement that lowered the antlers almost to back-level—and swung off with long, graceful strides. We were so

*"Could this striking pattern, plus the
two forward-thrusting lowest antler tines,
be a caribou's snow-glasses?"*

*A bull Peary's Caribou, interrupted while eating saxifrage blossoms,
strides gracefully upslope to another snowless stretch of tundra.
Photographed near the southern tip of Baillie-Hamilton Island
on 2 July 1969 by David F. Parmelee.*

close that we could hear the clicking of his dew-claws. Hardly had he got fairly under way when he stopped, looked us over again, and went after saxifrage once more. I was struck with the disproportionate bigness of his antlers and with the black area around each eye. I had to use my binocular, and look closely, in perceiving that the eye itself was only a small part of the facial blackness. Could this striking pattern, plus the two forward-thrusting lowest antler tines, be a caribou's snow-glasses? The idea seemed worthy of further thought.

As we approached the sea, the slope steepened. Now we were obliged to wade through knee-deep snow, broad strips of which paralleled the shore. The open ground was slippery and treacherous. Young Phil, eager to see the kittiwakes, shot ahead, following a narrow bare strip that led straight to the highest part of the cliff at the island's end. Where forced to cross ice, he hacked footholds. I, toiling far behind, began to be afraid. Not since a bad fall I had had in Pennsylvania in the spring of 1929 had I liked cliff work. Especially did I dislike watching someone else climbing. Knowing how utterly without fear Dave Parmelee was, and wondering whether Phil might be equally dauntless, I asked Stu to wait for me. When I caught up, I extracted from him a promise that he would not let anyone, Dave especially, do anything that was patently dangerous.

Then it was that I noticed the awesome bank of snow overhanging us. As I watched Phil chopping away I wondered how much of a jar might be required to loosen tons of that snow. All of it was wet, almost soggy. I was tremendously relieved when I sensed that both Stu and Dave, and finally Phil also, had decided that even if we did reach the cliff by this high route we would not see the part we most wanted to see. No, the proper procedure would be retracing our steps, descending the slope to its very bottom, and following the shore to the cliff's base. Ice at the ocean edge was thick and firm, but rough. The dark gray shore itself, now snow-free, would be a made-to-order path.

111

The colony was large and noisy. Recalling that the word *kittiwake* was said to be onomatopoeic, I listened carefully for it, but what I heard was syllables of a hundred other sorts shrieked, squawked, and cackled as the graceful birds came and went. Many flew in upwind from the east, carrying great hunks of nesting material in their bills. Not a bird was motionless. Those at half-finished nests were fondling or bowing to each other—if they happened to be mates—or jabbing viciously and hurling threats in all directions. I had observed breeding kittiwakes before, notably along the coast of Iceland, where I had looked down on them. Here I looked up, fervently hoping that if a dropping did hit me it would miss my face.

The cliff was one of the most dangerous I had ever visited. The talus was composed of rock-chunks from fist-size up. Chunks of this sort might fall at any time, now that the nine months of frost had done their work. Twice I saw a rock give way as a bird tried to alight. The whole precipitous end of the island looked crumbly. A broken-winged kittiwake that we found almost certainly had been struck by a falling rock.

Presently I had not only two thousand or so kittiwakes to watch, but three men also—one toiling up the talus, another picking his way along the foot of the vertical rock-face, another on the ocean ice, half-hidden by apparatus, recording the unremitting cacophony. Parmelee, now up a way on the cliff itself— I was half-sick as I watched him—clung to a projection with one hand and reached, reached, reached with his scoop-net in the other toward the lowest nest he could find. Alas, he was too early for eggs. Very few, if any, of the hundreds of nests were finished.

112

We were puzzled by our failure to see a single raven or falcon. Every large gullery I had ever visited in the arctic had had at least one pair of predatory birds in attendance, ready to dispose of weaklings, cripples, and unguarded eggs or chicks. Was this colony so new that the ravens and falcons had not learned of its existence? Had pesticides so cut down the new world population of peregrines as to force colonies of this sort to manage without help?

We saw the caribou again on our way back to the Otter. This time I made a point of examining some clumps of saxifrage that the bull had "grazed." What a paunchful of purple petals that caribou must have had inside him!

Harold Mordy was in no mood for banter when we reached the plane. The stern look he directed toward the approaching fog, then toward us, needed no verbal enforcement. We took off just in time, flew for an hour or so without a glimpse of anything aside from ourselves and that opaque, occasionally luminous, never-anything-but-malevolent woolly whiteness just outside the windows, swung gracefully around while descending, suddenly emerged, beheld the bright buildings of Resolute below us, and alighted—no whit the worse for wear, and many a whit the better.

At Resolute, where the air-traveller might be better off dead than without patience, the eight-day wait for the flight to Montreal would have been wretchedly anticlimactic had it not been for the ivory gulls. Having failed to find those elusive birds along the northern edge of the great archipelago and at the Baillie-Hamilton kittiwake colony, we had virtually dismissed them from mind. Sched-

113

uled to fly south by commercial jet on July 2, we had made a point of returning to Resolute in plenty of time. But the fog was bad. Word from Frobisher Bay—about half-way between Resolute and Montreal—was not encouraging. Fog was bad there too. Phil Taylor was to return to Bathurst for the rest of the summer, but flying was out of the question unless the fog cleared.

At one of those low moments when inactivity, futile discussion, enforced cheeriness, and resentment over mankind's powerlessness to control nature threaten, like an accumulation of gas, to explode, what should suddenly clear the air but young Phil's announcement that he'd just seen "two, perhaps more, pure white gulls" along the coast only a few miles from the building in which we were billeted. "They're ivory gulls," insisted Phil. "They can't be anything else. They're right near the Eskimo village." Incredulous, we fired questions. Phil's answers dispelled doubt. The gulls were white, very white. There wasn't a bit of gray or black or buffy brown in their plumage. They weren't extra large—only a bit larger than a kittiwake.

Someone drove us to the Eskimo village in the middle of the night. There, informed as to just where the birds had been seen, we patrolled the shore, disgusted and angered by the refuse everywhere—tangles of wire; rusty tools; remains of boats, sledges, and radios; bones of seals, walruses, foxes, and bears; bottles and cans; a big skillet; boots, socks, caps, and dresses; dog carcasses with leering grins on their faces. Red smears on the ice marked spots where seals had recently been skinned and cut up. A pervasive stench occasionally became stronger, as if suddenly released. Nothing seemed clean, nothing except possibly the ice beyond the narrow lead and the band of open sky above the northern horizon.

114

It was there among the trash that I saw my first living ivory gull—a snow-white creature indeed, and a scavenger. Flying, the bird was almost invisible against the whiteness of the ice and fog; as it drew closer I realized that its stubby black legs were easier to see than its head, body, and wings.

We must have seen seven or eight ivory gulls all told, never more than three at a time. I had a good shot at one and missed, much to my chagrin. Dave Parmelee shot one, and Stu MacDonald two. Dave's specimen I held alive in my hands. Its bill was of lovely pale shades of yellow, green, and blue. Its round, wide-open eyes were very dark, almost black, its facial expression oddly dovelike. Especially striking were its bright vermilion eyelids. That night, working under fluorescent light, I drew the head of an unskinned bird.

One fact about the three specimens was disturbing: each had a well defined featherless area on its belly, proof that it had been brooding eggs or young. We could not be very far from a breeding ground. Realization that nests might be within touching distance, so to speak, was maddening. But where would the nests be—on a cliff over the sea, on a small flat island, on a beach just above high-water mark? Would they be close together or widely scattered? Might they be among kittiwake nests, in a mixed colony? Questions of this sort bothered us sorely.

Especially annoying was realization that we could not travel far no matter how badly we wanted to find an ivory gull's nest, unless we were willing to change the summer's plans completely. There was no telling, no telling at all, when the jet would arrive. Dave Parmelee's face wore a pained expression. Harold Mordy, the Otter, and big maps became a part of every conversation. "Those little islands! Look at them!" argued Dave, pointing. "An ivory gull nest might

115

be right there right now, or there . . . or there!" The possibility could not be denied.

Came weather gloriously bright at Resolute and word from Frobisher Bay that the jet could not possibly get through because of fog there. "Yes," said Harold Mordy, "the Otter can land on Browne Island. You can have a look at the birds there. We ought to be able to take in some of those other little islands, too—at least have a look at them." Thus did it come about that we visited the big kittiwake colony on Browne Island—where glaucous and Thayer's gulls too were nesting—and flew over islets named Griffith, Garrett, Lowther, and Somerville. There wasn't time for Limestone, off the north end of Somerset.

Nowhere did we find an ivory gull's nest. But we did buzz a walrus. The great brute probably was napping when we first sighted it. Harold Mordy and the Otter obviously enjoyed the buzzing. The walrus, at first merely curious, became annoyed, then bewildered. Not knowing which way to turn, it rolled completely over before sliding into the dark water.

At Resolute the clear weather continued. Word reached us that Bathurst was fog-free too, so it was "Goodbye, Phil. Take care of yourself. Be sure to say hello to Dave Gray and the others."

As I watched the Otter becoming smaller, smaller, finally so small that it looked a little like a raven, coasting on set wings, I knew I was homesick. Homesick for my little academy on the Goodsir.

116

BIRDS MENTIONED IN THE TEXT

Red-throated Loon (*Gavia stellata*)
Brant (*Branta bernicla*)
Greater Snow Goose (*Chen hyperborea atlantica*)
Oldsquaw (*Clangula hyemalis*)
King Eider (*Somateria spectabilis*)
Gyrfalcon (*Falco rusticolus*)
Peregrine (*Falco peregrinus*)
Rock Ptarmigan (*Lagopus mutus*)
Black-bellied Plover (*Squatarola squatarola*)
Knot (*Calidris canutus*)
Purple Sandpiper (*Erolia maritima*)
Buff-breasted Sandpiper (*Tryngites subruficollis*)
Sanderling (*Crocethia alba*)
Red Phalarope (*Phalaropus fulicarius*)
Pomarine Jaeger (*Stercorarius pomarinus*)
Parasitic Jaeger (*Stercorarius parasiticus*)
Long-tailed Jaeger (*Stercorarius longicaudus*)
Glaucous Gull (*Larus hyperboreus*)
Thayer's Gull (*Larus thayeri*)
Ivory Gull (*Pagophila eburnea*)
Black-legged Kittiwake (*Rissa tridactyla*)
Arctic Tern (*Sterna paradisaea*)
Snowy Owl (*Nyctea scandiaca*)
Raven (*Corvus corax*)
Lapland Longspur (*Calcarius lapponicus*)
Snow Bunting (*Plectrophenax nivalis*)

MAMMALS MENTIONED IN THE TEXT

Arctic Hare (*Lepus arcticus monstrabilis*)
Varying Hare (*Lepus americanus*)
Collared Lemming (*Dicrostonyx groenlandicus*)
Short-tailed Weasel (*Mustela erminea*)
Barren Grounds Wolf (*Canis lupus arctos*)
Arctic Fox (*Alopex lagopus*)
Walrus (*Odobenus rosmarus*)
Peary's Caribou (*Rangifer tarandus pearyi*)
Muskox (*Ovibos moschatus*)

INDEX